Praise for *Reputation Design+Build*

"With a good reputation, you can recover from nearly anything. You could lose your big client, have a key employee turn into a fierce competitor, or suffer any number of financial setbacks – but you'll always come back. Where does that reputation come from and how can you build it? Scott Butcher is a really smart guy with many years working as a marketer and manager in the A/E industry. In his book, *Reputation Design+Build*, he lays out the path anyone can follow . . . . Good reading – I highly recommend it!"

>Mark C. Zweig
>Founder & CEO, Zweig Group
>Author, *Management from A to Zweig*

"Scott Butcher has always been a visionary and sooth-seer to the masses within the design and construction industry. Those who have been wise enough to listen to his message and follow the future he lays out ahead of them will win. We live in truly exciting and dynamic times with changes occurring daily. We have to all be nimble, innovative, and willing to try new processes outside of our comfort zone. Scott has provided in the book an excellent road map for you to follow. He has provided a clear strategy for building your reputation and ensuring a profitable and rewarding future for yourself and ultimately your company. Take the time to study this book. Make sure your fellow leadership read it also, as it can make you all successful and wealthy in the years ahead."

>Ronald D. Worth, CAE, FSMPS, CPSM
>CEO, International Association of Assessing Officers
>Former CEO, Society for Marketing Professional Services
>Co-Author, *Design-Build Services, A Marketing and Business Development Handbook* and *AEC Marketing Fundamentals*

"Scott's book is an excellent resource for any A&E professional that wants to up their game and take their career and platform to the next level. Every firm and individual should be looking for ways to differentiate these days, and Scott lays out clear cut strategies, tools and case studies proving how it should be done . . . . I highly endorse this important resource and urge everyone who wants to be hired for his/her talent and reputation to read this book and implement Scott's recommendations."

> June R. Jewell, CPA
> President, AEC Business Solutions
> Author, *Find the Lost Dollars: 6 Steps to Increase Profits in Architecture, Engineering, and Environmental Firms*

"Where Scott's book really shines is in helping you find and develop authentic alignment between your identity and image: the key to creating and sustaining personal brand value . . . . Follow his simple and straightforward steps – learn from the many anecdotal profiles of those who themselves have developed strong brands – deliver on your personal brand promise and your reputation, as well as that of the organizations you serve, will benefit. An excellent read for those seeking to understand and leverage the often under-appreciated concept of *brand* in professional services."

> Craig Park, FSMPS, Assoc. AIA
> Author of *The Architecture of Image: Branding Your Professional Practice*
> Past National President, Society for Marketing Professional Services

"*Reputation Design+Build* not only sounds a warning bell for A/E/C firms that desire to remain relevant, it also provides a highly detailed, step-by-step guide to creating that relevancy. In today's economic climate, particularly in the A/E/C market space, you simply cannot afford to be common or unremarkable . . . . The solution, as Scott effectively demonstrates, is to intentionally develop your own personal brand. *Reputation Design+Build* is easy-to-read and jam-packed with real-world case studies and concrete examples. If your intent is to become an industry leader with a powerful personal brand, this book is your ticket. Highly recommended!"

> Kelly S. Riggs
> President, Business Locker Room
> Author, *Quit Whining and Start Selling! – A Step-by-Step Guide to a Hall of Fame Career in Sales* and *1-on-1 Management: What Every Great Manager Knows That You Don't*

"This book shows Scott's depth of experience in marketing and business development in the A/E/C industry. It is an interesting and very personal look into what it takes to establish your brand, filled with analogies, anecdotes and personal reflections. To illustrate his points he has used no less than 16 in-depth case studies with A/E/C industry fellow professionals."

>Ernest Burden
>AEC Advisors
>Author, *Client' End Game: Innovative Strategies and Processes for Building a Client-Centric A/E/C Firm* and *Successful Project Management: For A/E/P and Environmental Consulting Firms*

"In the book, *Reputation Design+Build*, author Scott Butcher combines his first-hand knowledge of best branding practices with real life applications by other industry leaders. The result is a powerful step-by-step plan of action that if followed, will position any firm to win more business."

>Dana Birkes, APR, CPSM, FSMPS, FPRSA
>Chief Marketing Officer, Clifford Power
>Past National President, Society for Marketing Professional Services
>Past President, SMPS Foundation

"Add this book to your A/E/C Must Have list. Scott Butcher takes personal brand building for professional services to a whole new level. The tools are applicable, relevant and detailed. Beyond the tools are amazing references and case studies that truly exemplify the right way to make us all better, more successful professionals."

>Frank Lippert, FSMPS, CPSM
>Business Development Manager, Parsons Brinckerhoff, Inc.
>Founder/Co-Owner, Go! Strategies, LLC
>Past National President, Society for Marketing Professional Services

"Scott nails it with this book! It should be given to every employee at your firm to educate them on the state of our industry and help them develop their personal brand. Follow his recommendations, and you're set up for a successful career."

>Julie Luers, FSMPS
>Vice President, Director of Marketing, HGA Architects and Engineers
>Past National President, Society for Marketing Professional Services

"This book is the A/E/C industry's most comprehensive plan about building your professional brand. Whether a practitioner, marketer, or business developer, Scott's explanations, case studies, tools, and resources explain in depth what you need to know to position yourself for success. The Gap Analysis & Personal Marketing Plan will undoubtedly help the reader create a truly differentiated, personalized, and credible roadmap for professional excellence."

> Barbara Shuck, FSMPS, CPSM
> Firm-wide Marketing Communications Manager, Wilson & Company
> 2014-2015 National President, Society for Marketing Professional Services

"Scott Butcher is dead-on. Your personal reputation is just as critical to successful marketing and business development as that of your firm. Like it or not, we trade on our personal brands every day. I've seen it – both the good and the bad! – in my roles as project engineer, then principal, then CMO of my company. Scott hits on every point you need to consider when thinking about your career and, really, your life. Don't just read this book. Absorb it. And then act on it."

> Brad Thurman, PE, FSMPS, CPSM
> Principal & CMO, Wallace Engineering
> Past National President, Society for Marketing Professional Services

"This book is a practical guide to personal branding. Although the entire book is helpful, Butcher avoids the usual clichés with self-improvement books, and offers insightful case studies throughout. He hits upon the key to success early on with his discussion on attitude. Without the right attitude, the personal journey of reputation building is pointless. That advice early in the book caused me to pause and reflect upon my own attitude. This book will be a key component for me as I work to build my personal brand."

> Donna Jakubowicz, FSMPS, CPSM
> Midwest Marketing Lead, AECOM
> Past President, SMPS Foundation

"Scott Butcher's book, *Reputation Design+Build*, identifies what a personal, professional brand is and what it is not. He provides insight through individual case studies that underscore positive outcomes when you proactively manage your professional brand. This book is a must read for anyone in the A/E/C industry!"

>Carolyn Ferguson, FSMPS, CPSM
>Owner, WinMore Marketing Advisors
>Editorial Advisor, *Building Design + Construction* Magazine
>Past National President, Society for Marketing Professional Services

"When I was younger, my parents always said that a good reputation is one of the most valuable things that you possess. There was no resource for reputation-building at that time, but we now have a guide on how to nurture and enhance our reputations. Scott's insights on building a reputation are important for people in all phases of their personal and professional lives. My sons are both headed to college in the next year, and I plan to share a copy of *Reputation Design+Build* with each of them as they enter the professional world."

>Melissa Lutz, FSMPS, CPSM
>Principal, Champlin Architecture

"Having professionally practiced in the design and build business for 30 plus years, I am well aware of the impact my brand has had on my career. Scott has captured, in his book *Reputation Design+Build*, how your Brand gets developed, how critical it is, and how to perpetuate it. He supports his views by providing clear behavioral examples through Case Studies that will undoubtedly help evaluate and grow your personal Brand."

>Tom Townes, AIA, FSMPS, CPSM
>Director of Business Development, Van Note-Harvey Associates, PC
>Former President, Focus Architecture

"Scott Butcher combines ideas, examples, practical advice and tools in this must-read resource for A/E/C professionals. With the building design and construction industry becoming increasingly competitive, it's not enough to have great credentials. You've got to package your experience, expertise and knowledge. Butcher – who's done this for himself – walks you through how to build your own personal brand to enhance your reputation and stand out from competitors."

> Jean Leathers, CPSM
> President, Practice Clarity

"Scott Butcher not only gets 'it,' he does personal branding himself, mentors others on it, and shares his wealth of knowledge selflessly. This book is the perfect balance of tried and true, personal experience and tireless research. If you're in the A/E/C industry, you should read this book. If you're struggling to understand why others that are less technically proficient than you are rising to your company's upper ranks, you NEED to read this book now. Scott hands you the big picture, explains the tools necessary, and backs it all with case studies. If you don't do something soon, your competition for that next promotion, job, or project will."

> Perryn Olsen, CPSM, CCMP
> President, Brand Constructors
> Author, *Construction Executives Guide to Brand Marketing*

Reputation Design+Build

Creating Winning Personal Brands for Engineering, Design, and Construction Professionals

© 2015 by Scott D. Butcher

Published by Scott D. Butcher, www.scottbutcher.com.

All rights reserved. The text of this publication, or any part thereof, may not be reproduced in any manner whatsoever without written permission from the publisher.

Table of Contents

Praise for *Reputation Design+Build* 1
Table of Contents 9
Acknowledgements 13
Foreword by William Long, PE, LEED AP, FSMPS 23
Understanding Branding & Reputation Management 29
    Up Your Game 32
    What is a Brand? 37
    Can People Be Brands? 40
    Tom Peters & the Personal Branding Movement 43
    Reality: Personal Brands Are Still Different 46
    Times Are a Changing 51
    The Challenge of Being a Commodity 54
    Building and Managing Your Reputation 58
Tools Part I: The Baseline 61
    The Baseline: You 63
    The Baseline: Education & Training 68
        Case Study: Gary D. Anderson, PhD, AIA, FAICP, LEED AP 72
    The Baseline: Licenses & Certifications 75
    The Baseline: You're Only as Good as Your Portfolio 83
        Case Study: Carl Elefante, FAIA, LEED AP 94
Tools Part 2: Building Your Reputation 97
    You Know Your Community – Do They Know You? 100
        Case Study: John Klinedinst, PE 105

Leading Your Peers Through Professional Associations 108

    Case Study: Judith Nitsch, PE, LEED AP BD+C 114

Client Organizations: Making Your Prospects Want to Meet You. 117

    Case Study: William Johnson, CFM 120

Writing to Build Credibility 122

    Case Study: Holly Williams Leppo, AIA, LEED AP BD+C, NCARB, NCIDQ 131

    Case Study: Craig S. Galati, AIA, FSMPS, CPSM 133

The Power of the Podium 135

    Case Study: Scott W. Braley, FAIA, FRSA 147

Making News Instead of Reading It 150

    Case Study: J. Timothy Griffin, PE, CEM, LEED AP, CBCP 155

Virtual Reality: Knowledge Sharing & Networking from Your Office Chair 158

    Case Study: Daniel Kerr, PE 177

Expanding Horizons: Pro-Bono & Freelance Work 180

    Case Study: The 1% 184

    Case Study: James Abell, FAIA 185

Embracing Your Creative Side 187

    Case Study: Laurin McCracken, AIA, FSMPS 190

    Case Study: Christopher Brooks, LEED AP 192

Mentoring Your Replacement 194

    Case Study: Adam Snavely 197

Soccer Moms (& Dads) Bring Home the Bacon 200

Networks Above, Below & Beside 203

Table of Contents

- References & Testimonials 210
  - Case Study: Josh Carney, PE 215
  - Knowledge 217
  - Additional Tools 224
  - Combining the Tools 232
    - Case Study: Ardra Zinkon, IALD, MIES, LEED Green Associate . 238
    - Case Study: William Long, PE, LEED AP, FSMPS 240
- Gap Analysis & Personal Marketing Plan 243
- Appendix – Links of Interest 267
  - Organizations & Societies 267
  - Service Groups 272
  - Industry Publications 273
  - Training 276
- About the Author 277

Acknowledgements

This book would have not been possible without a lot of people, organizations, and publications.

For starters, my wonderful wife, Deborah Butcher, and our amazing son, Jonathan. Debbie has been very patient with me over the years as I've spent evenings and weekends writing books and articles, taking trips around the country to speak or attend conferences, and supporting me every step of the way. And Jonathan, well, he's our little miracle. Born fourteen weeks early and weighing a mere 19.2 ounces, he encountered challenge after challenge during his 124 days in the NICU. He's healthy, vibrant, and a lot of fun today, and I like to say that no matter what I accomplish in life, I'm always playing catch-up to him! Plus, he taught me how to blog, even though I didn't call it blogging at the time.

My parents, Marla and Don Butcher, have always been there for me and encouraged me. Perhaps by never discouraging me from trying anything they cultivated in me a belief of, "Yes, I can do that." I'm in this industry because of my father, who owned both an engineering firm and an architectural/engineering firm. When I was in college, he gave me an internship. And when I graduated, he gave me my first real job. Of course, I graduated during the recession of the early 1990s, meaning that job pickings were slim. I had three opportunities: sell forklifts, sell copy machines, or market engineering services. So of course I took the job that paid the least, because it was what I wanted to do: marketing. Many days I'm very thankful to Dad for getting me into the industry. Other days I curse him!

I've worked with Steve Jamison for two decades. At times he's been my dotted-line boss, at other times my direct-line boss. Steve is the kind of supervisor that everyone would want to have – one that lets you do "your thing" and always be trying something new. There have been times when I approached him to get his thoughts about a new opportunity before me, and he's responded, "Well, why *wouldn't* you do that?"

There are many tools in this book to help you develop your personal brand and enhance your reputation. Some of these tools require you to be out of the office – attending conferences or trade shows, presenting to industry or owner groups, networking over lunches and after hours. It is a lot easier to do these things when you know you have great support back at the office – someone who can run with things when you are not around. For me that person has been Sarah Gaenzle. As of this writing we've worked together for five years. It used to be that when I was out of the office she'd call or email me with questions or for direction. That practice stopped a long time ago because she is able to totally run the show in my absence! This book has a section about mentoring your replacement. I hope that I've done that with Sarah – I've been able to try and do so many new, interesting things because of her talents. Of course, she's probably now waiting for me to get out of her way!

You'll read about Bill Long in this book. He's been my friend and SMPS colleague/partner in crime for a lot of years. We've co-authored articles together and co-presented at local, regional, and

Acknowledgements

national engagements. Bill and I have presented together numerous times on the subject of reputation management, and his knowledge has greatly informed this book – in fact, we originally strategized the content for this book together. He opened the door for me to get involved with the SMPS Foundation. In fact, I followed him as president of the organization. Because we've co-presented together many times on the SMPS circuit, some of our colleagues like to joke about our *bromance*. But as you'll see when you read his case study, he's a renaissance man in this industry, and the rare technical professional that has made the transition from full-time doer to full-time marketer and business developer.

Speaking of SMPS, or the Society for Marketing Professional Services, I need to recognize the organization. When I was hired as JDB Engineering's marketing coordinator, I was a first for the firm. They never had a true marketer before me, and thus I was without a mentor. However, less than a year into my career, I found the organization, meaning that I had finally found my mentor. Our relationship spans more than two decades, and while I originally "took" from SMPS – that is, gained knowledge and valuable information – today my role is focused on giving back to the organization that gave me so much.

Over the years, I've been fortunate to have worked with a number of publishers who have been interested in what I've had to write. Periodicals that have published my articles include *The Military Engineer*, *PSMJ Best Practices*, National Electrical Contractors Association *Marketing Advice & Customer Relations Report*, *Pennsylvania Contractor*, SMPS *Marketer*, *Professional Services Management Journal*, *A/E Marketing Journal*, *The Zweig Letter*, *Writer's Journal*, and *Pennsylvania Magazine*. I'm grateful to the editors of these publications for giving me a shot and, often, coming back for more. I didn't realize it during the early years of my career, but they were helping me to establish my brand. In 2001, I packaged a number of my previous articles together, along with some new ones, and published *Market-

ing in the Building Industry as both an ebook and print-on-demand book. It's safe to say that I was a bit early to the party, as ebooks were certainly not ready for prime time! Back then an ebook was pretty much a PDF that you read on your PC, Mac, or laptop. There were no Kindles or iPads or iPhones at the time. In fact, phones were still dumb. But I did learn a lot about the publishing industry in the process and it served as a springboard from articles into books.

The York County Convention & Visitors Bureau, Main Street York and Genesis Publishing gave me the opportunity to try something new with my writing, and I ended up authoring and photographing seven visitors' guides and numerous relocation guides. A big thank you to Kim Scott Carl, president of Genesis Publishing, for opening a new world to me. A new passion in me was born, and soon I was researching, writing, and photographing local interest books. Arcadia Publishing, The History Press, and the York County Heritage Trust each published one of my books. But it was my relationship with Schiffer Publishing that was the most prolific. Together we've created eight books so far!

I also want to acknowledge James McClure, managing editor of the *York Daily Record*. In 2007, Jim asked if I'd be interested in blogging on the newspaper's blog platform, York Town Square. I wasn't sure if I should or could. But as we got to talking, I realized that I was already a blogger. When my newborn son was in the hospital, my wife and I found that we had neither the time nor the energy to update all of our family and friends about our day-to-day trials and tribulations during Jonathan's NICU journey. So at the suggestion of a nurse, I set up a Caring Bridge page, and updated it daily, writing in Jonathan's voice. It was a way to share important developments, and perhaps work through some of my fears as I was writing from the viewpoint of a tiny baby who didn't realize the severity of the situation. Well, when I told Jim about my Caring Bridge page, he said: "You're already a blogger!" For the next sev-

Acknowledgements

eral years, I contributed regular posts about history and architecture to York Blog under my personal blog, *Windows Into York*.

In 2012-2013, I was fortunate to be a part of something special with the SMPS Foundation. Working with my friend Scott Braley, FAIA, FRSA, we led a team of 29 intrepid researchers, writers, editors, and designers to create the book *A/E/C Business Development – The Decade Ahead*. It was a fun and occasionally stressful project that opened doors for me to speak about the research findings at locations near and far. Furthermore, I was able to greatly expand my network while presenting alongside some remarkable people!

My experiences with writing all these articles, blogging, and publishing more than a dozen books, through both the traditional model and self-publishing approach, greatly informed my ability to publish this title on my own. Yes, I could have worked with a traditional publisher, but in this case I really just wanted to be my own publisher, incorporating the myriad lessons that I've learned over the past twenty years.

I've been extremely fortunate over the years because people, and organizations, have been interested to hear what I have to say. With more than 200 presentations under my belt – not including client/prospect presentations or project interviews – I've learned to develop presentations and be comfortable in front of audiences. SMPS Central Pennsylvania (then an affiliate of the Philadelphia chapter) and SMPS Philadelphia gave me an early platform to present on things like marketing planning and project photography. Those early presentations were given with the aid of an overhead projector, pre-PowerPoint! But they opened the door to lead roundtables at the SMPS National Conference, and eventually become a local interest speaker in central Pennsylvania. Through it all, I've spoken to general business audiences, seniors' groups, community organizations, technical A/E/C professionals, and marketers of design and construction services.

Reputation Design+Build

I'm grateful to have been selected to speak at the national conferences and programs of SMPS, Associated General Contractors, American Council of Engineering Companies, NCSEA, PSMJ Industry Summit, and Society for Design Administration. I'm so fortunate to not only have presented multiple times to SMPS Central Pennsylvania and SMPS Philadelphia, but to have been invited to speak to the Maryland, Pittsburgh, Northeast Ohio, Greater Cincinnati, Chicago, Arizona, Columbus, Virginia, and Palmetto Chapters. I'm thankful to the SMPS Southern Regional Conference, Pacific Regional Conference, Heartland Regional Conference, Southeastern Regional Conference, and Northeast Regional Conference for the opportunity to present, as well as the AIA Central PA and AIA Philadelphia Chapters. These presentation opportunities have introduced me to an amazing network of people in our industry, and helped to further establish my brand and inform the recommendations and ideas in this book.

I'm a huge proponent of community trusteeship, or community service. Our communities are better places when intelligent, caring, and dedicated professionals join together to enhance our villages, towns, and cities through serving non-profit organizations. My early exposure to this concept was serving on the public relations committee of my local Boy Scout Council, but it wasn't until I attended and graduated from the Leadership York leadership training program that I really understood the needs of my community and the role I could play in helping it. Of course, my parents, Marla and Don Butcher, were always engaged in community nonprofits, so they paved a trail that I gladly followed! I served as a director on the boards of Leadership York, York County Convention & Visitors Bureau, American Red Cross – York County Chapter, Main Street York, and Historic York, becoming an officer in three organizations and the president of one. I've also been active with a number of other nonprofits, including the York County Heritage Trust, York March of Dimes, and William Goodridge Freedom House &

Acknowledgements

Underground Railroad Museum. As you'll see in this book, I believe that community engagement is the "low-hanging fruit" of reputation building, and I'm so blessed to have been selected as a *Central Penn Business Journal* Forty Under 40 as well a Leadership York Outstanding Alumnus of the Year, in no small part because of my efforts in the community.

Service to one's profession is a critical aspect of personal brand-building, and I've certainly been able to leverage involvement with a number of organizations to help me advance my career and benefit my firm. I previously mentioned my involvement with the Society for Marketing Professional Services. In 1993, I joined with Betty Helms, Don Banzhof, Ed Stetz, Ron Hoover, Donna Smith, and Diane Dunn Pickel, later joined by Robin Zoufalik, to create the Central Pennsylvania Chapter of SMPS. We were perhaps not ready for the big show, so we were established as an affiliate of the Philadelphia Chapter. It was here that I really found my footing in my profession and began building what has become an amazing network of friends. I spent six years on the governing committee, serving as secretary, membership chair, and sponsorship chair. This opened the door for me to become involved with the SMPS Philadelphia program committee and serve as the chapter newsletter editor for several years.

After I moved on from local SMPS service, I was fortunate to serve several stints on the National Certification Committee. Eventually I was approached by the SMPS Foundation to serve as a liaison between the Foundation and their white paper authors. Fortunately, the white paper I was assigned, after a bit of lobbying on my part, was *The Client's Use of Social Media and Networking*, authored by Holly Bolton, Dana Galvin-Lancour, and Adam Kilbourne. It was such a great experience, and they taught me so much about using social media within the A/E/C market space. I was later elected to serve on the SMPS Foundation Board of Trustees, serving first as Thought Leadership Committee Co-Chair, followed by Secretary,

President-Elect, and President. It has been an amazing experience working with the A/E/C industry's marketing and business development thought leaders. Mike Reilly, Rhodes White, Bill Viehman, Jan Tuchman, Scott Braley, Donna Jakubowicz, Dana Birkes, Kelly Riggs, Steve Isaacs, Bill Long, Diane Rutledge, Lisa Roberson, Holly Bolton, Julie Luers, Michelle Fitzpatrick, Larry Casey, Taree Bollinger, Larry Gramlich – these are the fellow Trustees with whom I've had the honor to serve. Their leadership and extensive knowledge have certainly greatly impacted me and made me a better professional services marketer because of my interaction with them! You probably recognize many of their names – they are speakers and authors and consultants and editors. They have elevated the profession and provided insightful guidance to countless A/E/C professionals.

Through my involvement with the SMPS Foundation, I've also benefitted greatly from spending time with a number of recent SMPS Presidents. They too are industry thought leaders, and their tireless leadership and commitment to enhancing the profession of marketing and selling professional services has raised the bar and informed the content of this book. They include Frank Lippert, Kevin Hebblethwaite, Brad Thurman, Carolyn Ferguson, Barbara Shuck, and Paula Ryan.

I also need to acknowledge the unbelievable dedication of SMPS staff. First and foremost, former SMPS CEO Ron Worth was everything you could possibly want in a chief executive leading more than 6000 marketers and business developers in advancing the profession. He is the most positive person that I've ever met, an amazing cheerleader for everyone who crosses paths with him, and a friend that has encouraged me to do more and think bigger. Thanks for the push, Ron! Michele Santiago and Molly Dall'Erta have been there for me and the SMPS Foundation, helping to push things forward and keeping things moving between meetings. A special shout-out to Tina Myers, Mary Cruz, Kevin Doyle, Dan

Acknowledgements

Reilly, Lisa Bowman, Mark DellaPietra, Linda Smolkin, Jaime Flores, and other staff members past and present, who have kept a well-oiled machine at SMPS, helping tens of thousands of professionals advance their careers over the years.

As I was in the final stages of completing this book, an exciting new opportunity presented itself. I have the honor of being the voice of my profession *and* representing SMPS on *Engineering News-Record's* website, ENR.com. Thank you Jan Tuchman and Richard Korman for the awesome opportunity!

Finally, a big shout-out to Barbara Neff, who proofread every word of this book to ensure that even though it is self-published, it would still come across as having been professional published.

If this Acknowledgements section sounds partially like a biography, it should. There's a method to my madness. So congratulations if you have read this far! As you will see when you read this book, a lot of the content in this Acknowledgements section relates directly to the tools for building and maintaining your reputation. Many of these tools relate to becoming a subject matter expert (SME). And to become an SME, you need credibility. I have a close relationship with the various tools that I've outlined. I've tried them all, with varying levels of success. I truly believe that each and every tool can be extremely effective as you begin your journey to becoming a branded professional in the A/E/C industry. I've experienced first-hand what these tools have done for me. Although I refer to personal experience throughout the course of the book, it was more important to me that you see the successes of other professionals from using these tools; thus the many case studies that I've included. But I became a subject matter expert at using these tools because of the many opportunities and personal experiences of the past twenty-five years. Many people and organizations have helped me along the way, and I thought it important to acknowledge them and also provide some background as to my

Reputation Design+Build

personal experience with using these tools to build my own reputation.

An important lesson here is that while you, and only you, control your brand, you can't go it alone!

Foreword by William Long, PE, LEED AP, FSMPS

When I graduated from college over thirty years ago and first entered the design and construction industry, I would often look to the people in the profession that I considered "successful." Presidents of large architecture/ engineering firms. Executives with international construction management companies. Sole practitioners that were at the top of their game. Were they good designers? Did they manage subcontractors the best? Maybe. But it soon became apparent that they were not necessarily in their position of responsibility and power because they were a great designer or a great builder.

Yet these individuals commanded the respect of their clients, peers, and co-workers. People admired them and wanted to work with them. This translated into an accelerated career path, increased revenues for their companies, and the establishment of a firm culture at their firms that reflected their leadership ability.

But why did some individuals attain this status and many others did not?

As I reflected on this, I also tried to understand why I and others actually thought so highly of these individuals. Personally, some of the primary reasons that I thought they were considered successful included the facts they were featured speakers at industry conferences, they were quoted in client publications, they possessed specialty certifications, or they were active participants in their community.

I did not fully grasp the linear relationship between these activities and the individual's status but I knew these activities were behaviors that I needed to emulate in my career! In fact, these behaviors were something that I acknowledged were necessary but I was not able to verbalize their specific impact on a person's career nor even put all the pieces together in a cohesive plan for personal growth.

But Scott Butcher did.

Scott and I had known each other from early in our careers in the building industry. As our careers continued to develop, my professional relationship and personal friendship with Scott strengthened. He and I would have semi-regular discussions about this topic (and others), often over breakfast or a cup or two of coffee, and it was apparent that Scott knew what he was talking about. He referenced how individuals in other professions had personal brands and talked about how they managed their reputation. He applied that same thought process to the A/E/C industry and referenced individuals that embraced these behaviors and firms that embraced these concepts. He also correctly pointed out that these individuals were not always the partners of firms or presidents of companies. They were the project managers, the estimators, the project engineers, and the designers.

Personally, I just felt that "this is what I should do" and assumed I was supposed to do it. However, others do not necessarily

Foreword by William Long, PE, LEED AP, FSMPS

feel that way and need to be shown why and how. One of Scott's greatest attributes is his ability to teach. He is able to break down concepts into their most prominent attributes, recognize the benefits of certain behaviors, relay them via anecdotes, and accurately predict results. With his insight into reputation management in the A/E/C industry, he did what I anticipated he would. He selflessly started helping others develop their own personal brands.

Through informative presentations, personally-developed worksheets, and real-life case studies, Scott was able to convince co-workers of the need to develop their personal brand. More importantly, he has been able to successfully train and coach them along this process. Together, Scott and I then jointly presented these concepts to peers in our industry organizations and also co-authored articles on the topic, thereby expanding his reach within the industry.

However, with this book, Scott takes his knowledge and approach to the A/E/C masses. In fact, the greatest advantage of reading this book is that it is a great opportunity to learn from the master. He is able to concisely relay – via specific suggestions, case studies, and examples – what I have seen work for individuals in various roles within the building industry.

I personally have embraced the concepts that are presented while managing my own personal reputation and I am proud to say they work! After thirty years of experience, I can honestly say that they have helped to define my career, led to financial opportunities, and provided me with a great deal of personal and professional satisfaction.

Today, I am surrounded by other individuals in the design and construction industry that also embrace their personal brand. Architects leading in their community. Engineers being recognized as experts. Construction managers getting certifications. All of these individuals are now reaping the personal and professional benefits of their actions. Read this book. Follow Scott's lead. Embrace his suggested actions. And you will be one of those individuals who successfully develops their own personal brand and manages their personal reputation.

> William R. Long, PE, LEEDAP, FSMPS
> Principal, Vice President
> Canuso Jorden, Inc.

Foreword by William Long, PE, LEED AP, FSMPS

"It takes twenty years to build a reputation, and five minutes to ruin it. If you think about that, you'll do things differently."

- Warren Buffett

"We make a living by what we get, we make a life by what we give."

- Winston Churchill

"Who are you, 'cause I really want to know, tell me who are you?"

- The Who

Understanding Branding & Reputation Management

"Today, we hear about architects becoming 'brands.' In our profession, brand is simply a short word for 'reputation.' A good friend of mine described reputation as, 'What people say about you behind your back'."

– J. Robert Hillier, FAIA, PP

Bob Hillier has created quite a powerful personal brand in the design and construction industry during his decades of practice. He founded Hillier Architecture, a firm that won more than 300 design awards. He received the Michal Graves FAIA Lifetime Achievement Medal from the American Institute of Architects and was recognized by *INC Magazine* as New Jersey's "Entrepreneur of the Year." The Professional Services Management Association awarded him with the first DaVinci Award for Excellence in Leadership.

While Bob was winning design awards and personal accolades, he was also sharing his knowledge as an instructor at the School of Architecture of Princeton University. He was serving on boards and committees of organizations large and small. He was a sought-after speaker, even speaking at the United Nations. He was branching out, becoming majority owner of *Princeton Magazine* and Princeton's *Town Topics* newspaper. Although Hillier Architecture merged with RMJM Group in 2007, the reputation that Bob established has carried him through to the next phase of his career, and he is still recognized as one of the most successful architects in the United States. In fact, he still practices architecture with the firm he founded with Barbara Hillier, Studio Hillier.

Bob Hillier did all the right things to create a powerful international brand, and his company prospered because of it.

Not everyone is Bob Hillier.

Of course, not everyone is you, either. In fact, there is only one of you. And, as it turns out, you are quite valuable: to your employer, to your community, to your industry, to your clients, to your family, and to your friends. Yes, there is only one of you. That is why this book is about *you*.

But why should you care about personal branding and reputation management? After all, they're just abstract business terms thrown around by marketers and a bevy of consultants who want to help you part with your money by "building" your brand.

Believe or not, your reputation is your calling card. Your reputation will help you gain and maintain employment. It will help you grow a new firm or bring in work to an existing one. It will gain you recognition in places you never thought possible. These benefits alone should make you sit back and take notice.

Clients of design and construction firms have become pretty sophisticated. They're onto us – they know the games we play to embellish our credentials: promoting projects that were completed years ago or, worse, completed by *former* employees of a firm. They can see through the marketing smoke and sales mirrors. They want to know about you. They are increasingly selecting design and construction firms based upon the strength of individual team members (well, that and cost, but that's a whole other book...). They are looking for the weakest link. Don't be the weakest link!

Karl Speak, co-author of *Brand You*, sees a clear distinction between professional services firms and product oriented firms: "Making brand personal with everyone in the firm is fundamental to brand building in professional services."

What do we sell in our industry? We sell hours. We sell people. We sell the knowledge of the architects and engineers and surveyors and estimators and project superintendents and construction managers.

And guess what? Our owners and clients want to know that each team member is an All Star. It doesn't matter how large or small their project happens to be: it is important to them – it is their world – and they want to know, *need* to know, that the A-Team is working on their project.

If you are not a member of the A-Team, you need to be, and fast. During the downsizing that began with the onset of The Great Recession, the C-Team found themselves unemployed. And in the years following the "end" of the recession, many members of the B-Team were given their notices. The design and construction industry is forever changed.

Up Your Game

If you don't believe it, here are some examples from design and design-build requests for proposals (RFPs).

> "Resumes for individual employees of the AE/CM and any design partners' key personnel that the AE/CM intends to employ on this Contract. It is mandatory that previous food or beverage experience be demonstrated by each key resume. Include three personal references for each team member."
> – Food Manufacturing Project RFP

> "The architect must be a licensed architect, LEED AP, and have served as Architect of Record for a LEED Certified project. They must also have demonstrated experience as lead architect for design-build projects in the $5 million to $10 million range, completed within the past three years."
> – Federal Project RFP

Here's one that recently came across my desk for a design-build Indefinite Delivery – Indefinite Quantity (IDIQ) contract. The client had minimum requirements, and then gave additional scoring points to those who exceeded these requirements. Here's an overview of what was needed:

- All design and construction personnel were required to have at least ten years of industry experience *performing the role* for which they were being proposed. So a project manager with ten years of experience as a site superintendent and five years of experience as a construction project manager was not acceptable.

- Preference was given to a construction project manager with a four-year college degree in architecture, engineering, or construction management.
- Preference was given to a design project manager with a four-year college degree in architecture or engineering plus a valid AIA or PE license. Note that they didn't ask for a Registered Architect (RA), but instead wanted an RA with AIA credentials. Furthermore, this individual received higher scoring points in they had twelve or more years of experience leading multi-discipline design teams.
- The site superintendent received higher scoring if he or she had at least fifteen years of experience as a superintendent (ten years was required).
- The quality control manager, in addition to being required to have at least ten years of experience in quality control, received additional scoring points if he or she had at least five years of experience in the commissioning of major building systems.
- Additional points were awarded to any team member with experience managing projects that included sustainable design features and LEED certification.
- Resumes for design and construction team members had to include "up to" five relevant projects. A relevant project was defined as:
    - At least $500,000 in construction cost
    - Project entailed repair and alteration of occupied and functioning building space
    - Project involved repair and alteration of one or more building systems including architectural, structural, mechanical, electrical, fire protection, and life safety

- The project was completed within six years of the issuance date of the RFP
- At least two of the projects must have been completed using design-build project delivery
- While the criteria above were required, the owner agency also laid out additional criteria to earn extra scoring points with regard to relevant projects. These included:
  - Project involved repair and alteration to a historic building
  - Project required close coordination with occupant's/owner's security requirements
  - Project demonstrated challenges in staging materials and site access
  - Project involved sustainable design features and LEED requirements
  - Project involved installation of special security spaces such as vehicle and personnel screening
  - Project involved installation of telecommunications infrastructure
- For the design team members, additional points could be earned if they demonstrated:
  - Tangible evidence such as certificates, awards, peer recognition, etc., demonstrating design excellence
  - Advanced professional degrees
- For the resumes, each project description for design team members was required to include:
  - Design approach with salient features
  - How the client's program, functional, image, mission, economic, schedule, and operational objectives were satisfied by the design or planning solution

Understanding Branding & Reputation Management

- Client reference including name, title, address, email, phone, and fax numbers

To add insult to injury, this RFP also dictated that the entire proposal could be no more than 80 single-sided pages (no duplex printing allowed), using Times New Roman typeface in 12 point size. White 8.5" x 11" paper was required, with one inch margins on all four sides.

So not only did this agency have some extremely detailed requirements for each team member, if you happened to submit their resumes with the wrong font or point size, the entire team would be disqualified. Sometimes I read requirements like these — which are increasingly common — and feel like the profession has devolved to *Romper Room*. Are we that much of a commodity that in order to differentiate us clients must base decisions on proposal font choice?

As a marketer of professional services, I'm seeing more and more examples of language like this in RFPs. In the case of the first example — the food manufacturing project — they didn't even ask for relevant projects of the firm much less references of the firm. It was all about each individual team member. You can't hide behind the smoke when the clients are analyzing your staff in depth. Veterans of the industry are used to not getting projects because of fees or construction costs. We're used to not getting projects because the competition had better credentials or, as a colleague of mine frequently says, "They had more poker chips than we did." However, now we have another reason for not getting work: "Your civil engineer only designed four projects in the municipality — the other person had done six." Or, "Your architect was licensed and a LEED AP, but the other firm had an architect with LEED AP BD+C." Or, "Your construction manager doesn't seem to be very involved with the profession, and we felt more comfortable with someone who was a leader to her peers."

Furthermore, when it comes to those pesky shortlist interviews, the design and construction professionals are on their own, too. "Kindly leave your marketing and sales staff back at the office" is a quote directly from a letter notifying my firm that we had been shortlisted and scheduling an interview.

As John Perez, Vice President of Cumming Corporation, told a large audience of A/E/C marketers and business developers at Build Business 2014, "Bring your subject matter experts to interviews. Speak directly to the audience and their topics." An executive from a commercial real estate development firm echoed this in the SMPS Foundation book, *A/E/C Business Development – The Decade Ahead*: "I would much rather talk to an engineer who is thirty years into his or her career and is now focusing on new business generation, promoting his or her firm, and knowing the business thoroughly, rather than a person hired solely for new business that has never actually executed a project. I am wowed by the solid business expertise and the enthusiasm and energy behind someone who believes in what they do."

Just how important are the people to a project? Some clients are now requiring firms to essentially *guarantee* that the proposed design or construction team will be involved throughout the life of the project.

Understanding Branding & Reputation Management

What is a Brand?

So exactly *what* is a brand, other than a kind of laundry detergent or potato chip?

The American Marketing Association (AMA) defines brand as "A name, term, design, symbol, or any other feature that identifies one seller's good or service as distinct from those of other sellers."

While that might mean something to a marketing professional, it really isn't that helpful when trying to expand the concept of branding to people – save for one word: *Distinct*.

Another definition is, "The single concept you own in the mind of the prospect." This is still somewhat abstract, but probably brings us a little closer to where we are headed.

This "single concept" is really based upon an association. If you read or hear the name of a well-branded product, you probably automatically have an association for it. That association – attribute, description, whatever it may be – is known as a category. Here are a few examples:

Safe car

What do you automatically think of? Volvo. Some Volvos are fast. Others are roomy. Some people might even find Volvos stylish. But they are known first and foremost for safety. More to the point: if you are in a bad accident, you will survive. (This is known as brand promise.)

Fast food for kids

Your immediate association is probably McDonald's – and they are really the only option here. Think Happy Meals, playgrounds, and a clown mascot. Wendy's targets adults, Burger King goes after the 15-30 year-old males. McDonalds owns kids, which means that McDonalds owns families. That's why they are a Top 10 global brand.

Achoo! Get me a…

Complete this sentence. Did you think tissue? Or Scotties? Or Puffs? Most of us would say Kleenex. It is such a powerful brand that it has become generic. Do we really have a preference toward the particular manufacturer of the tissue? This has happened with other branded products, too. For instance, do you still make Xerox copies? (On a Konica Minolta or Lanier copier?) Or ask for a Band-Aid when you cut yourself? Do your children ask for a gelatin dessert? Of course not – they want Jell-O! They just don't care which company actually manufactures it.

Original cola

I once asked this question at a presentation and someone responded "RC." But most everyone else associates original cola with Coca-Cola; after all, it is the "real thing." So how powerful is Coca-Cola as a brand? They are perennially ranked as one of the top three brands in the world by Interbrand. They *own* the word "cola." Their primary competitor, Pepsi, was actually called Pepsi-Cola, but dropped the "cola" in 1961 because Coke and cola are synonymous, even though Pepsi is a cola. Ironically, in 2014 Pepsi created a new product using sugar instead of high fructose corn syrup. Because it is essentially a throwback product, they decided to name it Pepsi-Cola, perhaps trying to capitalize on the brand link between "cola" and "original."

There are examples of this in our industry, too. Sometimes the brand association is with a type of project or building. But this association may only be for a certain geographic region.

What comes to mind when you think of a firm that designs and builds power facilities? Probably Bechtel, which you may also associate with petroleum or transportation. How about a firm that designs water facilities? Tetra Tech.

The next example is a trick question. What firm in our industry is "all things to all people?"

I actually heard a nationally-recognized consultant to our industry, speaking about the importance of focus, say: "You can't be all things to all people ... unless you are AECOM."

With 95,000 employees, as much as $20 billion in annual revenues after their acquisition of URS, offices throughout the world, and the #1 design firm designation on ENR's annual rankings, they sort of can. But they are the exception, not the rule.

What about a design firm that focuses on sports facilities?

There was once a time that most people automatically thought HOK Sport+Entertainment. But the firm – no longer part of HOK – is now known as Populous, and they have a broader mission, which is "to create environments that draw people and communities together for unforgettable experiences." As a company, they've had a branding challenge: new name, broader focus. Interestingly, HOK decided to get back into the world of sports and entertainment design with the 2014 acquisition of 360 Architecture.

Can People Be Brands?

These examples, however, don't answer a fundamental question: can people be brands?

Here's another definition of brand, from *Brand Aid* by Brad VanAuken: "The sum total of each person's experience with your organization." I really like this one, and it brings us closer to our destination, because it begins to make things personal. This is a broad definition, of course, meant to apply to products and services. But at the end of the day, isn't that what the design and construction industry is all about? Personal experiences; personal interaction.

So here's one final quote that I've come across, and it hits the nail on the head: "Half of your brand is created by the marketing department; the other half by customer service." So at the end of the day, a marketing department can promote your company a certain way, but the real test of your brand is how you interact with your clients. Each and every team member has the power to reinforce a corporate brand. Or destroy it.

The brand association test also works when applied to people.

There are many successful business tycoons, but only one really has his name stamped on *everything*.

Donald Trump.

How about someone who is famous for simply being famous?

Paris Hilton. Kim Kardashian.

Who is *the* lifestyle mogul?

After all these years, it is still Martha Stewart (although she has a lot of competition these days).

And yes, there are even examples in our industry. Modern architecture? I.M. Pei. Deconstructionism? Frank Gehry. Prairie School? Frank Lloyd Wright. Romanesque Revival? H.H. Richardson.

Granted, we have moved from the era of the branded architect to the branded architectural firm; however, individual architect brands are making a reemergence.

Understanding Branding & Reputation Management

So we know that products can be brands, companies can be brands, and famous people can be brands. But how does that apply to you? Are you a brand? And, if so, when did you first become a brand?

For some of us, it may have been an association with a larger group or organization, like Scouting. You may be familiar with the Scout Law. "A Scout is Trustworthy, Loyal, Helpful, Friendly, Courteous, Kind, Obedient, Cheerful, Thrifty, Brave, Clean, and Reverent." Aren't these attributes that we mentally apply to a Boy Scout? We also know what a Boy Scout isn't – how many times have you heard someone misbehaving told, "You're no Boy Scout!"

If you didn't have a brand association before high school, chances are you belonged to a clique in high school. Think *The Breakfast Club*, which was both a movie about the perceptions we hold about someone identified with a certain group or clique, as well as an emphatic point that people – yes, even high school students – are broader than one "clique."

In the movie, the students were serving detention on a Saturday, and their assignment was to write an essay about who they are. Throughout the course of the movie, they interacted and learned more about one another, going from strangers to friends during the course of the detention. At the end of the movie, "The Brain" wrote an essay for the group, addressed to the teacher:

> "Dear Mr. Vernon, we accept the fact that we had to sacrifice a whole Saturday in detention for whatever it was we did wrong. What we did WAS wrong, but we think you're crazy to make us write an essay telling you who we think we are. You see us as you want to see us ... In the simplest terms and the most convenient definitions. But what we found out is that each of us is ... a brain ... and an athlete ... and a basket case ... a princess ... and a criminal. Does that answer your question? Sincerely yours, The Breakfast Club."

Look in a mirror. How would you describe the reflection staring back at you?

That is not your personal brand. Remember Bob Hillier's quote about brand/reputation at the beginning of the book: "What people say about you behind your back."

In personal branding – or reputation building and management – the more appropriate question to ask is, "How would others describe you?"

However, the different people you know in life would probably describe you differently:

- Social Media Connection
- Family Member
- Friend
- Co-Worker
- Supervisor
- Industry Colleague
- Community Contact
- Client
- Former Co-Worker

Your reputation may, in fact, precede you; however, that reputation may vary from person to person. So how do we create a positive, consistent reputation that will enhance our career? Cue the personal branding movement...

Tom Peters & the Personal Branding Movement

There are various versions of the origin of the personal branding movement. Certainly, the concept is as old as time – Napoleon, George Washington, Abraham Lincoln – they all had personal brands. Heck, you can go back even further. Original sinner? Adam.

Napoleon Hill's 1927 book, *Think & Grow Rich*, may have planted the seed for reputation building and management. However, the popular book *Positioning: The Battle for Your Mind*, by Al Reis and Jack Trout, is frequently cited as the birthplace of the personal branding movement. What is this so-called movement? It is simply an attempt to control how others perceive you by embarking on a series of strategic actions. The book is primarily about positioning companies, but there is a chapter dedicated to "Positioning Yourself and Your Career."

It is an article from the December 18, 1997 issue of *Fast Company*, written by management guru Tom Peters, which really launched the concept into the mainstream. Peters wrote:

"Regardless of age, regardless of position, regardless of the business we happen to be in, all of us need to understand the importance of branding. We are CEOs of our own companies: Me Inc. To be in business today, our most important job is to be the head marketer for the brand called You."

Elsewhere, Peters writes:

"You don't belong to any company for life, and your chief affiliation isn't to any particular 'function.' You're not defined by your job title and you're not confined by your job description. Starting today, you are a brand."

From this article, an entire industry was launched. Search an online bookstore and you'll find myriad titles about personal branding or reputation management, each with its own spin on the concept. Titles include *The Brand You 50 (*by Tom Peters, incidentally), *The Brand Called You*, *Me 2.0*, *Managing Brand You*, *Career Distinction*, *Be Your Own Brand*, *The 10Ks of Personal Branding*, *Personal Branding for the Business Professional*, and more. Each author has a different area of focus. For some, personal branding is for executives building companies. For others, the concept is reserved for job hunters and college students. And yet for others, a personal brand is something defined by social media use.

The concept is now omnipresent. YOU were *Time* magazine's person of the year in 2006 – even if you didn't know it. From an accompanying article: "Treating our personalities as products reflects an increasingly competitive society in which the best way to stand out is to develop an engaging – and easily identified – image.

The Wall Street Journal, *Fortune Magazine*, *Harvard Business Review*, and *Inc.* are just a few of the publications that have promoted the concept of personal branding or reputation management. In *Fortune*, the concept was promoted as a way to keep your job: "Today, at a time when jobs are scarce, successful employees working at large companies desperately need to create a 'brand within a brand,' a professional passport that travels with them from place to place."

In Peter's groundbreaking article, he suggests that there are a number of ways to build your brand. These include moonlighting within your organization (taking on new responsibilities), freelancing outside of your organization, teaching at a local college or providing company training, writing a column for a local newspaper or company publication, and participating in a panel discussion or giving a presentation at a conference.

Peters believes that there are four measurements of your effectiveness:

- Be a great teammate and supportive colleague.

- Be an exceptional expert at something that has real value.
- Be a broad-gauged visionary – a leader, a teacher, a far-sighted "imaginer."
- Be a businessperson – be obsessed with pragmatic outcomes.

Reality: Personal Brands Are Still Different

I'm a big fan of the concept of personal branding: just not the terminology. It sounds abstract and even egotistical. Plus, there are some major differences between a "brand" and a "personal brand." For starters, a brand – by definition – is singular. However, you are multi-faceted. In high school, maybe you were an exceptional athlete or you wore preppy clothes or were smarter than everyone else. You were pigeonholed as a jock or preppy or nerd. But there was more to you back then, and there certainly is much more to you now.

Furthermore, brands are narrow. McDonald's is a corporation that is: (1) for-profit, (2) in the restaurant business, (3) with a fast-food focus, and (4) a target market of children and families. That's pretty narrow. You, on the other hand, are well-rounded. You have multiple areas of focus, strength, interest, and personality.

Beyond this, personal branding sometimes suffers from being too focused on a specific career level or activity. For instance, personal brands aren't *just* for job seekers – but they can help a job seeker stand out from their competitors for a position. Likewise, they aren't *just* for executives – although the most successful businesspeople have built their businesses around themselves. Personal brands also aren't *just* about your online activities – although channels like blogging and LinkedIn and Twitter are great tools for creating a specific perception people may have of you (positive or negative, by the way).

In the branding vernacular, marketers commonly use two terms: personality and promise. Brand personality is exactly what it seems like – and the definition of personality as you know it is actually a good way to look at your reputation. Is your personality one of an introvert or extrovert? Are you always willing to share knowledge or do you keep it close to the vest? Do you dominate a conversation or listen and ask questions? Are you friendly or grumpy? This is all part of your personality. When dealing with reputation and personal branding, personality is simply what distinguishes you. How would someone describe you? What makes you distinct?

Promise, or — in this case, brand promise — is simply what someone should expect from you when dealing with you. Earlier in the chapter we looked at the effectiveness of branding for products and companies. When asked the question, "What is a safe car?" you most likely immediately thought of Volvo. Volvo's brand promise is that if you are in a really bad accident, you will live. That is powerful. A close friend of mine was hit head-on by a drunk driver in a police pursuit. It is a miracle that he survived, yet he did, and has the scars to prove it. It took multiple surgeries and a long period of recovery. Guess what he was driving? A Volvo. And guess what he does today? He is the sales manager for a Volvo dealership. Talk about brand promise — every breath he takes is literally a demonstration of Volvo's brand promise in action.

In personal branding, when someone knows about you (because of your reputation — either one that you've carefully built or one that is based upon what people say about you behind your back), they have a general idea of what it would be like to deal with you. This holds true whether at the office, in the community, or as a coach on your kid's sports team.

There are many attributes that define your personality. Here are a few:

- Leadership
- Knowledge
- Influence
- Innovation
- Value
- Network
- Self-Esteem
- Authenticity

- Education
- Follow-Through
- Confidence
- Image
- Passion
- Communication
- Experience
- Appearance
- Relationships

If we meet and spend any amount of time together, at the end of the day there is probably one thing that I'll remember about you more than anything else: your passion (or lack-thereof). What are you passionate about? What motivates you, gets you fired up, or makes you smile? And if you yawn and look disinterested during the meeting, well, that says a lot about your brand, too.

My daughter was born severely premature, and only lived 90 minutes. Two years later, lightning struck twice, and my son was born severely premature. He weighed just one pound, three ounces and was only twelve inches in length. My wife and I spent the next 124 days in the NICU by his side, day in and day out. He's smart, healthy, thriving, and the only lingering effects of being born fourteen weeks early are occasional bouts of asthma. Needless to say, my wife and I feel unbelievably blessed. We saw a lot of heartache in the NICU, and families that were never able to leave the hospital with their little preemies. We could relate firsthand to their pain. But we also saw phenomenal teamwork from the amazing York Hospital (PA) NICU team. There is simply no way that we could ever repay them – I'm a dad to a healthy child because of them.

So what do you think I'm passionate about?

Get me talking about the NICU and our experience there and I'll probably tear up. But I'll do it with a smile, because I get to go home every day and hang out with a miracle! One of the ways my

Understanding Branding & Reputation Management

family is able to give back is through the March of Dimes. We were Ambassador Family for our local March for Babies one year, and my wife and I served as Revenue Co-Chairs for the event another year.

You have your own similar passions – we all do. And most of us have multiple passions. Everyone knows the Golden Rule – "Do unto others as you would have them do unto you." But do you know the Platinum Rule? It is, "Treat others in the way they like to be treated." The Golden Rule is about you, in a sense – it makes the assumption that others prefer to be treated the same way you prefer to be treated. The Platinum Rule, however, is all about the others. So if you know someone's passions, you have a direct line to their heart and soul.

Chris Brogan, a social media expert and author of several best-selling business books, wrote an ebook, *Personal Branding for the Business Professional*, which is a free PDF available on his website, www.chrisbrogan.com. In it he writes:

"Passion is what fuels the best of what we do. It's that tireless drive to do something that we feel matters that will bring us forward in so many ways."

Marketing professional services – architecture, engineering, construction management, interior design, environmental, etc. – is far different than marketing products. Cars are designed and tested and redesigned and retested and it can take years between original concept and the manufactured car reaching an automotive showroom near you. Professional services – which is an overarching category that also includes attorneys, accountants, and doctors, to name a few – is all about the people providing a service to other people.

As a marketer of professional services for more than twenty years, I've often referred to myself as a personal brand builder. And while I do work to develop my own reputation, my job requires me to build the reputations of my co-workers. Almost every marketing material has a reference to someone's personal brand – cover letters, professional resumes, proposals, websites, emails, presentation introductions, and more. Often, a professional is positioned as an expert based upon their education, license, and experience. A version of this sentence has been written literally millions of times by thousands of design firm marketers:

Jim Miller, AIA, LEED AP, a licensed architect with more than two decades of experience, is an expert in the planning and design of biomedical research facilities.

The names change, the facility types change, but the sentence remains the same. The author of this sentence – or the introducer at a presentation or interview – is actually branding the person. In the example above, the audience or client now fully expects Jim to know everything that there is to know about planning and designing biomedical research facilities. After all, he is an expert. His brand has been established and a perception created.

In smaller firms, Jim's expertise may *change* by the day, depending upon the project being pursued. Maybe on Monday Jim is the research facility expert, but a proposal on Wednesday establishes Jim as an independent living facility expert and by Friday Jim's brand is as a widget manufacturing facility expert. When you sit back and look at it, this approach becomes almost laughable. The "brand promise" is created – clients know what to expect – but there may be little or no credentials to back it up.

Karl D. Speak, co-author of *Be Your Own Brand*, is keenly aware of this. He writes, "The overarching importance of personal relationships is the distinguishing feature that makes brand building different for professional services firms." Elsewhere in his white paper, "Leveraging the Power of Personal Brands to Build a Stronger Professional Services Brand," Speak states: "The underlying structure of any professional services firm's brand is the 'personal brands' of each of the members of the firm. The brand equity of a professional services firm is the sum total of the personal brands of all the associates (employees)…"

Times Are a Changing

There was a time when professional services marketers could get away with marketing only a firm's credentials and project portfolio. If we had a relevant project, it would become the cornerstone of our qualifications statement, proposal, or presentation. Whether or not any of the staff members who had worked on it were still with the firm was irrelevant. Whether or not it was two decades old was irrelevant. Whether or not the client contact from that project was still there – or even accessible at all – was irrelevant.

But somewhere along the way, clients became more savvy. They began hiring design and construction professionals who knew the game that all firms were playing. Requests For Proposals became more restrictive. Even the Federal Government moved beyond their archaic Standard Forms 254/255 and created a new Standard Form 330, which required A/E firms submitting for Federal work to identify ten example projects (often completed within the past five years), proposed team members, their project role, and whether or not those team members actually worked on the ten example projects. For those of you familiar with the Standard Form 330, it is known as Section G – the bane of many marketers' existence! I've submitted what I thought were many strong SF 330s, with lots of checks in the Section G, only to be told by contracting officers during debriefings that we were disqualified because we didn't have enough checks in the columns!

This focus on the individual components of a team coincided with another global trend: connectivity. In the 1990s, everyone got email. Many people also got cellular phones. In the early days, they were quite large (my first mobile phone was a "bag phone" that was actually larger than any phone in my home). We entered a new millennium, and these mobile phones began getting smaller and smarter. We could text on them. Then we could get on the Internet. Then we could use them for email. And suddenly social media began popping up all around us, too. MySpace – well, that was for the kids. Facebook – that was a bit more intriguing, but had a "personal" focus. Some of us became involved, often becoming "friends" with people we hadn't seen or spoken with in decades (high school reunion on Facebook!). But businesses began to take notice of social media, and soon there was a major new social media channel being launched every month. Today, most of us have at least a LinkedIn account. We Tweet, we Pin, we upload photos to Instagram, we post videos to YouTube, we Skype, and we hang out online in Google Hangouts. Oh, and we can do this all on our smartphones.

There used to be two entrances to reach us: the door to our office and the door to our house. We lived different lives from 8 am to 5 pm, Monday through Friday, than we did from 5 pm to 8 am weekdays and on weekends. Professional life. Personal life. Limited connection between the two.

But these separate lives have blurred, and now there is little differentiation. We are in contact 24 hours a day, seven days a week. We write emails minutes after waking and right before we go to sleep. We check out social media sites day and night – it could be work-related at home, or personal-related at work. Often it is both. Every day. A whole generation – the Millennials – is demanding this freedom and accessibility. And Generation X, increasingly moving into senior management roles, is often leading the charge. Savvy Boomers are caught up on the train. Fuddy-duddy Boomers (you know a few, admit it – but if you are reading this book and a member of that generation, you are not one of them!) are tired of being agents of change and revolution, and now are looking forward to comfortable chairs and retirement.

So we have a juxtaposition of two major trends. Professional services firms are increasingly relying on the reputations or personal brands of their employees, while everyone in every role is increasingly accessible. Whether you like it or not, you are being

Understanding Branding & Reputation Management

Googled. People are researching you on the web. Maybe it is a vendor trying to find out about you before their first meeting. Perhaps it is an organization looking for volunteers. Possibly it is a potential client who is trying to determine whether or not the perception created by your firm's marketing materials is "real" or just smoke and mirrors. Perchance it is a potential employer checking up on you before offering you a job. Conceivably it is someone in media looking for an expert to contact for a story.

As one owner told the SMPS Foundation in their book, *A/E/C Business Development – The Decade Ahead*, "Today, we are so busy, that more often than not, we might make the first contact with an A/E/C firm. We do reference checking and online research."

The worlds have collided and one thing is certain: you are in far greater control of your destination than you have ever been before. So stop following the road, and blaze your own trail!

The Challenge of Being a Commodity

Unfortunately, there is third major trend, and it is unfavorable for design and construction professionals.

You are a commodity. (Don't take offense; marketers have been viewed as a commodity since marketing was invented.)

Many clients and owners simply can't differentiate between one firm and another, or between one engineer and another. So they act like a buyer of commodities, and purchase the product with the lowest price.

You can't blame the clients: we have trained them. I recall a presentation about A/E websites. The presenter had studied more than 100 such sites, and concluded that 90% of them were "roughly the same." Same layout. Same sections. Same wording. To a visitor, these sites were essentially indistinguishable.

The same can be said for marketing materials, presentations (particularly the ones with really bad PowerPoint!), advertisements, and trade show booths.

My company does a significant amount of work in the food and beverage industry, and several years ago we were shocked when a stock photo we used appeared at two other competitors' booths at a trade show! If you work in industry, you know that it is sometimes more difficult to get a camera on the production floor of a manufacturing plant than it is to get a camera into a government facility! Firms that work in this arena are often forced to use stock photos, and it's not like there are thousands of readily available images. Still, it was quite surprising (sadly amusing, in fact) to see competitors using the same graphics. But what kind of impression does that leave on the purchaser or user of design and construction services? "These firms are all the same."

Physicians get paid very well for their services. So do accountants. There's a plethora of attorneys, broken into those that can barely scrape by and those that charge $300 or $400 per hour for

Understanding Branding & Reputation Management

their services. Why pay that rate? Because they've effectively branded themselves as the lawyer that you need – you are willing to pay their rates because you want to work with them. You need them.

But how does this apply in the design and construction industry? My father founded a successful engineering firm as well as a second architecture/engineering firm, and often told me that "This isn't the business to get into if you want to be rich."

That especially holds true after The Great Recession. We've gone the other way with fees. There once was a time that a general rule of thumb was that a full-service design fee should be 6% of construction cost for a new building, and 8% of construction cost for a renovation. Then, because of various complexities, the fees began rising. But construction firms saw a void in the delivery of the traditional "construction administration" services performed by design professionals, and seized it. Construction managers entered the equation, and design fees began declining. Then the recession hit, and excellent firms with long traditions and impeccable reputations found themselves withering on the vine. Some folded; others were bought out or merged. The "survivors" began slashing fees. The traditional 6% became 5%, and then dropped from there. There are many anecdotes of projects going for 3% or less of construction cost, meaning that the design firms are actually working at a loss just to keep staff busy.

In the process, we've retrained our clients. They've come to expect lower fees. Client loyalty has plummeted. Sure, they want to work with you because of your long-term relationship, but there is always another firm willing to work for a lot less. And hey, by the way, have you been overcharging your clients all these years? Once you drop your fees, they begin to wonder. And even where you have an amazing relationship and multiple client advocates, there is that dreaded *four-letter* word that is actually ten letters: Purchasing. Is anyone else tired of hearing, "I really want to work with you, but I'm required to get three fees (or bids)?"

As an industry, we've made ourselves a commodity. Mr. Generic, meet Ms. Generic.

And it hasn't just affected the design side. It may have hit architects and engineers first, but it didn't take long for construction firms to find themselves on that slippery slope. Many firms were established by hard bidding work, and then elevated themselves to a place where they were able to negotiate with their clients and leave that hard-bid world to others.

But remember, the clients and owners are much more business savvy than they used to be. Thoughts of loyalty have been replaced with the realization that "it's a buyers' market out there." Firms that thrived on negotiation – in some cases with long-term clients – have suddenly been thrust back into the world of bidding (and beating down their subs). Often, it has been a hard lesson to learn – the competition isn't just undercutting you, but doing so at prices that make it almost impossible to compete.

"But the client gets what he or she pays for."

We've all been rallying around that little plea for decades, but what has it changed? Okay, maybe you get a project on the backend. You lose the million dollar fee, but get hired for a $15,000 study to determine what went wrong. Has the client actually changed their behavior?

The truth boils down to this: the design and construction industry has created a business model that is simply not sustainable.

Ask anyone who has been in this industry for years: "Are you having fun?"

That's probably the one complaint I hear more than any other. "This industry just isn't fun anymore."

I hear it from architects and engineers, construction managers and site superintendents. I was at an A/E/C networking event and overheard a construction firm owner tell a young engineer-in-training to run far away from this industry and never look back.

Actually, when U.S. architectural employment declined by 30%, and national media began identifying architecture as one of the most overrated professions (*U.S. News & World Report*) and fifth most useless college degree (*The Daily Beast*), I was hard-pressed to find any architect with a smile on his or her face.

Many young professionals have left the industry, never to return. A colleague once referred to this as the "lost generation of architects." And yet, despite the business development challenges of the recession and its aftermath, there is a workforce shortage that is only predicted to worsen. Remember, the unemployed design and construction professionals are rarely part of the A-Team. So if you are on the B-Team or C-Team, there's a way back: build and manage your reputation. Create a new you.

Building and Managing Your Reputation

Why should you care about reputation management and personal branding? What does it mean to you? To answer those questions, simply look at the potential outcomes that come from being well-known as an innovator, thought leader, or one who provides information and value:

1. It helps to market your firm – whether you are the owner or a lower-level employee, your personal brand is a key component of the overall marketing program. In fact, in 21st century professional services marketing, each team is only as good as its weakest link.
2. It increases recruiting opportunities – if you are known, people will want to work with you or for you. This applies to the senior executives, department managers, project managers, and even younger staff, who may also be an important part of the recruiting process.
3. It enhances your career. Expanding your education, building your portfolio, gaining leadership positions in industry and client organizations, speaking, writing … these can only elevate your career, whether you plan to spend the next two decades with your current firm, look for a new employer, or hang your own shingle.
4. It makes you indispensable. During and after The Great Recession, I heard a lot of corporate executives saying that the economy created a good excuse "to get rid of the dead wood." A well-branded professional is not just live wood, they are a growing tree with new branches sprouting daily – both inside and outside the firm. That's job security.
5. It makes you sought-after. Companies will recruit you to work for them. Clients will seek you out to work on their projects. So not only will your firm see you as a peak

performer, but they will also realize that it is in their best interest to keep you engaged, challenged, and happy.

6. It expands your network. Your network gains you referrals, new opportunities, projects, friends, and more. Your network helps define who you are while also paving a trail for bigger and better things to come.

7. It allows you to gain knowledge. What you know is a key component of your reputation. People want to work with thought leaders, not thought followers. And the first step of the process is to gain knowledge (education, project experience, research, etc.) that you can apply to your job and your profession.

8. It allows you to share experiences. Successful networkers know that the key to building and maintaining a vibrant network is giving. When you have accumulated knowledge, you can share it through writing and publishing, speaking, and helping others. Your personal brand will never reach its peak until you enter this stage.

Tools Part I: The Baseline

The heart of this book is the Tools section, which provides effective, proven techniques that you can utilize to build and maintain your reputation. These *tools*, as I refer to them, are actually the same tools that you can use to develop business. There is overlap between the tools, and most successful design and construction professionals actually use multiple tools and are effective at repurposing and maximizing their efforts. So they might use an article they've written as a presentation topic for a professional association or client organization meeting, where they are also able to expand their network.

However, there is a "price of admission," and that is education, licenses and certifications, and a portfolio. Why is this the price of admission? Because the clients expect it. They assume that if you are going to be working on their project, that you already have the proper education, licenses, and relevant project experience. This is what I call the baseline. However, part of the process of building

Reputation Design+Build

your reputation is making sure that you don't just have the credentials, but that you have the **correct** credentials for where you want to go.

Of course, there is even a more basic tool – one that is so critical but often so overlooked: You.

The Baseline: You

Confused? Isn't this whole book about you? Of course it is. But before you are ready to move forward with the tools, you must first look in the mirror and make sure the person you see is ready to do this.

The journey of reputation building begins with your attitude. Do you really want to do this? Do you see the value in doing this? Or is this something that you feel obligated to do or something that was thrust upon you by a supervisor or colleague? If you truly don't want to enhance your reputation in a positive way that benefits your firm and career, than read no further. You have to *want* to do this. Building and maintaining a brand requires a lot of work – work that often takes you far beyond your normal comfort level. Do you have the right attitude?

Your attitude is something that is always with you. When given a new assignment, how do you react? When required to work evenings or weekends, do you complain or try to get out of it? When you are talking about other people, do you focus on their positive attributes, or are you quick to criticize?

I once worked with a colleague that had one of the worst attitudes a person could have. He thought he was surrounded by idiots. The company leaders were incompetent. Anyone attending a meeting with him clearly wasn't as smart as he was. Every attempt at strategy was a waste of time. All attempts at team building or company social events were a totally useless endeavor. He sat in meetings with a scowl on his face. If you watched him long enough, you were bound to see him roll his eyes, look off into space disinterested in the conversation, or shake his head in disagreement. On his best days, he was merely a jerk.

We've all worked *with* people like this. Hopefully you are not currently working *for* a person like this (perhaps it is time to look for work elsewhere…). Regardless of how successful someone like this is — how good they are at their job — the reality is that their reputation will always proceed them, and not in a positive way.

The moral of this story is that if you try to implement some or all of the reputation-building tools in this book, you will fail if you aren't a pleasant person! If you aren't nice to the people you work with and the people you meet along the way, your accomplishments will be ignored and people will remember how negative you are about everything. That will be your personal brand. As you read through the description of my former colleague, you probably pictured someone from your own past (or present). Just as when someone says "safe car" you think Volvo, when someone says "negative jerk" or something like that, you have a brand association with someone you know.

Appearance is another overlooked tool, and it includes everything from your attire to your cleanliness to your breath and body odor. How sad is it that I feel obligated to write this? But we've all been out at events, and had to shake the hand of a slob with questionable hygiene and really bad breath. He or she could be the most talented person in their field, but is that what we remember? No, we remember how they dressed or how they smelled. Now I'm not an expert on what goes on behind the women's restroom door, but I can recall countless times where I've been in the men's room and witnessed a perp (police speak for perpetrator, or one who commits a crime) fail to wash his hands after completing his *task*. Now, do you really think that I want to shake his hand afterward? I've heard that it takes at least ten positive impressions to overcome a negative impression, but I'm pretty sure eleven meetings later I'm still going to recall the lack of hygiene!

How you shake hands says a lot about you, too. Everyone knows about the "limp fish" handshake, but the "over-squeeze" is equally offensive. If you over-squeeze my hand and cause me pain, I'm apt to avoid you at future events to spare having my hand and finger bones compacted into half their normal state. Likewise, the vigorous handshake, which entails rapid up and down movement, is best avoided. Just be firm and match the grip of the other person.

Openness is another key. You have to be open to trying new things — knowing that some will fail — and meeting new people. You have to be open to suggestions and even criticism. You have to be open to sharing your knowledge with others, viewing your competitors as future teammates, and giving more than you get in return.

Professionalism may sound obvious, and yet the overall professionalism of the industry — and other industries — has declined. Voice mail and email have made it easy for us to avoid conversations. How many times have you needed to have an important conversation with someone, but were afraid of confrontation and instead called the person when you knew they wouldn't be there so you could leave a voicemail? Or, even worse, just sent an email?

How good are you at managing your email? This is an area where I'm lacking. Email can be overwhelming, and it often seems to be like climbing a mountain with no peak. So I, like many other people, respond to the most important emails. And then I let the other ones drop off my screen, and eventually forget about them. Shame on me! There are people out there expecting responses that never come. I know that I'm probably the rule more than the exception, but that is no excuse. Do you promptly follow up all emails sent to you?

The quality of writing in email has become so terrible that it has spread beyond the digital world into everyday written communications — and even conversation. Some people think punctuation is optional and electronic jargon is totally acceptable for conversations. OMG, I so don't think so!

Dress is less professional than it used to be. The design and construction industry has traditionally been less formal than other industries — who wants to survey existing conditions of a boiler room dressed in a nice suit? – but even those standards have relaxed in recent years. The Millennial generation wants to dress more casual, and many companies have obliged. Don't get me wrong, I've never been a big fan of the man-scarf (also known as a tie).

Professionalism is in the eye of the beholder when it comes to building and maintaining your reputation. It may be totally acceptable to write informally when emailing friends (although it is habit-forming, and should be avoided) and dress in jeans some days. But you must always know the audience with which you will be interacting, and if you don't know your audience, err on the conservative side.

Use proper English when writing emails, paying attention to the rules of grammar. If you know the person you are emailing – even if they don't write professional emails – that's no excuse to not write properly. You never know to whom your email will be forwarded, and it is far better to be safe than embarrassed. We've all been in the situation where we were mortified to see that our email recipient had responded but copied others, sharing our original content that was only meant for one person's eyes. Assume that any email will be read by others. And for what it is worth, don't be *that* person – the one that forwards personal or private emails to others. If there is important information that you would like to share, first gain approval from the author of the email.

Likewise, if you know you will be going out of the office – to a client office, to an organizational meeting, wherever – dress professionally. You never know who will be there. This doesn't mean that you need to wear a suit or dress as if you are going to a job interview. It is usually better to err on the side of being overdressed than underdressed. There is absolutely nothing wrong with "professional casual" as a dress code, but that doesn't justify old jeans and a tee-shirt.

Not everyone shares your belief of what is or isn't professional, and it is vital that you don't present yourself to others in a less-than-flattering light. Even within your own firm, just because you can dress casually doesn't mean you should. If you and a co-worker are true equals, and both are up for a promotion but only one of you will be selected, it is these seemingly little things that will make the difference. Maybe you are both talented engineers, but one of you dresses and writes professionally, and the other is a little sloppy at both. Both of you will stand out – one positively, the other negatively.

Finally, authenticity is the cornerstone of Brand You. You must always be authentic. Don't try to be someone you're not. Don't feign interest in something that isn't important to you. Be genuine at all times. It is an admirable trait that will make you likable and trustworthy. That stated, always be truly interested in what someone else has to say to you.

If you pass this first test, then it's time to move through the rest of this Baseline section to make sure you can live up to the expectations that your clients have already set for you.

The Tools:

- Attitude
- Appearance
- Handshake
- Openness
- Professionalism
- Authenticity

The Baseline: Education & Training

To become professionally-licensed in most states, you need to obtain a degree from an accredited institution. American architects, for instance, must hold a professional degree in architecture from a program accredited by the National Architectural Accrediting Board (NAAB). Less than 125 colleges and universities in the United States hold this accreditation.

Educational requirements are becoming more stringent, even moving toward requiring master's degrees to obtain professional licenses. The "Raise the Bar" initiative of the American Society of Civil Engineers is focused on increasing the educational requirements for those wishing to become licensed Professional Engineers. Soon, a bachelor's degree may not provide enough education to sit for the civil professional engineer exam.

Your educational achievements are part of your reputation, but they are a baseline. Clients expect that you have obtained the proper training in your profession – and this is often outlined in Requests For Proposals. For instance, "The fire protection engineer shall be a registered professional engineer, have a minimum of five years of experience dedicated to fire protection engineering, and have a degree in fire protection engineering from an accredited university." I've increasingly seen language like this in RFPs; however, there are quite a few licensed fire protection engineers that did not study fire protection engineering in college. Even though they are highly qualified and experienced, they are not eligible for the contracts because they do not meet the educational requirements.

What are the most stringent educational requirements for your discipline or function? If they are more advanced than your current level of education, then it is incumbent upon you to advance your education so you aren't left behind as requirements for licenses, certifications, and Requests For Proposals become even more stringent.

If you hold a professional license or certification, you most likely are required to obtain continuing education credits prior to applying for license or certification renewal. Most states mandate this for professional licenses, and most certifying organizations also require continuing education.

There are countless opportunities to obtain education – some free, some quite expensive. If you hold multiple licenses or certifications, you have a challenge in that you may have to obtain double the professional development hours because a CEU (or PDH or LU) for one license/certification may not apply to another. Some states and organizations allow firm administration courses (management and marketing) to count toward the requirement, while others prohibit it.

Most professional associations offer continuing education courses that count toward meeting the requirements of their certification programs. If you attend a few conferences, you may earn enough units (which are typically defined in hours) to meet your renewal requirements.

Many magazines offer continuing education units as well. Read an article, complete a short questionnaire to prove you read it, and submit it. Then they will send verification for your records. The same thing holds true for webinars – at the completion of a webinar you'll often be given the option to obtain a certificate verifying your attendance.

Organizations like PSMJ and Zweig Group also offer focused continuing education courses. Their programs range from project management to firm administration, the latter including management, business development, human resources, and marketing. Some of their programs may not count toward your CEU/PDH/LU requirements; however, these programs may lead you down a different career path by providing valuable education that will help you reach your goals. Many professionals are content to continue doing what they are doing, just get better at it. Other professionals want to make the jump to another position, like becoming a project manager or department manager or vice president, so these courses provide a valuable tool for enhancing your career and reputation, even if they don't count toward your continuing education requirements.

Through Dale Carnegie and Toastmasters programs you can learn to be a better manager or speaker. From SMPS you can learn or sharpen your sales and marketing skills. At client-related conferences and industry trade shows you can develop and further your brand as an expert at a certain type of project or a certain kind of building.

The primary focus of this tool is to obtain the necessary education, most often a degree, to allow you to practice your profession. Your clients automatically expect that you've obtained the proper education, and ongoing continuing education, to qualify you to work on their project. As you advance in your career, you may find that your path takes you in a different direction than your original training, so another degree may be required, or perhaps a specialized certificate program to showcase your education.

Colleges increasingly have construction management programs, something that really didn't exist two decades ago. So a lot of today's experienced construction managers don't have the same education as younger CM professionals, who may be degreed in the discipline. But as this younger crop of CMs move into various roles with owners and clients, the RFPs will increasingly require key members of a construction management team to have specialized degrees — much as with the fire protection engineering example listed previously, which is a relatively new development in the profession.

This targeted education may be required to meet the baseline — that is, your clients' expectations. Or it may be required for you to make the jump to another role, be it lateral (another technical discipline) or vertical (management, for instance).

There is another tool very closely related to education – I refer to that one as "Knowledge" – and it is covered at the end of the tools section, because while education is typically a course or degree program, knowledge is an ongoing activity.

The Tools:

- o   Bachelor's Degree
- o   Master's Degree
- o   Professional Association Conferences
- o   Professional Technical Association Programs
- o   PSMJ
- o   Zweig Group
- o   Dale Carnegie Program
- o   SMPS
- o   Client-Related Conferences
- o   Industry Trade Shows
- o   Industry Magazines
- o   Books & Videos
- o   Blogs

Case Study: Gary D. Anderson, PhD, AIA, FAICP, LEED AP

Gary studied architecture at the University of Southern California, earning a Bachelor of Architecture. He embarked upon a career that found him gaining an interest in the planning portion of design and construction projects, and he was able to further his studies at the University of Southern California, earning a Master of Urban Design. That was followed with a Diplom, the equivalent of a Master of Arts, from the International Graduate School at the Stockholm University. Gary later enrolled in the Whiting School of Engineering at Johns Hopkins University, earning a PhD in Geography and Environmental Engineering.

Gary is a licensed architect, LEED Accredited Professional, and Fellow of both the American Institute of Certified Planners (AICP) as well as the Society of American Military Engineers (SAME). Through the educational process, and countless continuing education projects along the way, Gary has been able to build a brand through his education. Today, his portfolio includes project experience in more than 30 countries and a reputation as the "go-to professional" for planning military facilities and completing Form 1391, a common element in the military construction process. In fact, today Gary is an architect/planner with the Defense Health Agency's (DHA) Facilities Division.

While most people tend to view education in terms of technical benefits, Gary frames his benefits in terms of communication: "I think being able to talk to people in different disciplines, as one of their own, is a big plus. I'd like to think that I'm comfortable speaking with architects, engineers, economists, and social scientists, as well as others in the liberal arts." Gary has been both a student and a teacher in foreign countries, and he thinks these experiences have further enhanced his communication skills. For instance, he taught in Saudi Arabia and found that "Although classes were taught in

English, many students were not very fluent in what was for them a second language. It was important to use very basic — but always correct — English and to try to eliminate jargon, even when discussing fairly technical subjects."

Among all of Gary's accomplishments is something that not many of his business colleagues know. During his final year of architecture school, Gary won a graphic design competition. Although the competition was originally for the Container Corporation of American, Gary's design has evolved into the universal recycling symbol known to millions of people throughout the world. He took his $2,500 in prize money to further his education at Stockholm University. How strong is Gary's reputation? He's one of the few people you'll meet who actually have a Wikipedia article about their career.

Next Steps:

1. Determine "gaps" in your education, and research training opportunities to help you reach your goal.

2. Investigate specialized degree-granting programs that will enhance your credentials for a specific field or industry.

3. Research senior-level, university-based continuing education programs, typically of short durations, that will hone in on one area or skill where you need to enhance your knowledge.

4. Review applicable periodicals. What are your clients reading? They expect you to be reading the same publications, too.

5. Be a sponge when it comes to professional and industry conferences. Attend as many as feasible (financial/time constraints). Enhance your skills through training from professional organizations, and then better learn your

clients' industries by attending their trade shows and conferences.

6. Mine data from industry websites. Can't make a conference? Perhaps the presentations and hand-outs are online. Certainly additional information is available regarding trends, forthcoming events, activities of the industry's movers and shakers (companies and people), and more.

The Baseline: Licenses & Certifications

If you are an architect, and need to seal drawings, than you need to be licensed. That's fairly obvious. There used to be a time when firms had one or maybe two licensed professionals in each discipline, supported by a team of non-licensed staff. But today, clients are looking in depth at the credentials of each and every team member. If the only licensed staff your company has are the owners or executives, they'll see right through that and know that *their* team members – those staff members assigned to their project – don't have the proper qualifications.

As evidenced in the first section of the book, today's Requests For Proposals drill down to each team member's individual qualifications. So if they require a licensed architect, they fully expect that the licensed architect listed in their proposal will be involved with their project from the beginning to end.

But often, that license alone is not enough. They want the architect to also be a LEED Accredited Professional. There are a lot of licensed architects with LEED AP behind their names. However, clients now often want a specialty, so they are looking for licensed architects with LEED AP BD+C. The field narrows with each requirement. One of the sample Request For Proposal statements presented in the first chapter of this book further required the licensed architect to not just hold a LEED AP (often BD+C), but also to have served as architect of record for at least one LEED certified project.

Clients are looking for certified construction specifiers to handle specifications. And certified commissioning agents to oversee LEED commissioning. And certified professional estimators to handle construction cost estimating. And ASHE (American Society for Healthcare Engineering) certified professionals to build their hospitals. Increasingly, these certifications are not value-added, they are required: the price of admission. These professional licenses and certifications were first common in the design professions, but have become widely used in the construction profession as well.

Licensed professionals will often say that they do not need these certifications because they hold professional licenses and thus they are already well educated and experienced as it relates to a particular certification. However, if the client is requiring a certification as part of the RFP and the professional doesn't have it, they simply aren't eligible to be on the team. In fact, these certification requirements are having a huge impact on go/no-go and teaming decisions.

Several years ago I was involved with a pursuit for a large government contract. The project solicitation (a four-page paragraph in 8-point font!) requested licensed and/or certified team members in more than a dozen categories, including industrial hygiene. One of the nation's largest environmental firms was part of the team, and they supplied resumes for several industrial hygienists. We had a winning Standard Form 330, the user agency wanted our team, and it seemed as though the stars were aligned for us. Imagine our shock when we found out that we weren't even shortlisted! As it turned out, one of the members of the selection committee disqualified our team because it didn't include a Certified Industrial Hygienist (CIH), which is a designation awarded by the American Board of Industrial Hygiene. The RFP did not specifically ask for a CIH, and the environmental consultant was absolutely sure that their staff members met the RFP requirements because they held the proper OSHA certifications. There are two lessons here. First, even though you *think* you have the proper certification doesn't necessarily mean you do. Second, always know what the client really wants – even if it seems obvious.

You're an expert or you want to build your reputation as an expert. So what licenses and certifications must an expert in your field possess? What are the clients requesting or requiring when they look to hire an expert in your field? What credentials do your colleagues and competitors possess?

Perhaps more than any other industry, the design and construction industry is filled with licenses and certifications, abbreviations and acronyms. It seems that every year several new certification programs become available. Below is a list of most (but not all) of the various certifications held by professionals in the A/E/C industry. How many of these apply to your area of expertise?

American Society for Healthcare Engineering

> Certified Healthcare Constructor
> Certified Healthcare Facility Manager

Associated Air Balance Council Commissioning Group

> Certified Commissioning Authority

American Society of Heating, Refrigerating and Air Condition Engineers

> Building Energy Assessment Professional
> Building Energy Modeling Professional
> Commissioning Management Process Professional
> Healthcare Facility Design Professional
> High Performance Building Design Professional
> Operations and Performance Management Professional

Building Commissioning Association

> Certified Commissioning Professional
> Associate Commissioning Professional

Reputation Design+Build

American Society of Professional Estimators

    Certified Professional Estimator

Society of Cost Estimating and Analysis

    Certified Cost Estimator/Analyst

US Green Building Council

    LEED Green Associate
    LEED Accredited Professional
    LEED AP Building Design + Construction
    LEED AP Operations + Maintenance
    LEED AP Commercial Interiors
    LEED AP Neighborhood Development
    LEED AP Interior Design + Construction

International Code Council

    Certified Code Safety Professional (multiple categories)

Construction Manager Association of America

    Certified Construction Manager

Institute of Certified Construction Industry Financial Professionals

    Certified Construction Industry Financial Professional

Tools Part I: The Baseline

Construction Specifications Institute

    Certified Construction Documents Technologist
    Certified Construction Specifier
    Certified Construction Contract Administrator
    Certified Construction Product Representative

American Society of Plumbing Engineers

    Certified in Plumbing Design

Association of Energy Engineers

    Certified Energy Manager
    Certified Sustainable Development Professional
    Certified Energy Auditor
    Certified Business Energy Professional
    Certified Energy Procurement Professional
    Distributed Generation Certified Professional
    Certified GeoExchange Designer
    Certified Residential Energy Auditor
    Existing Building Commissioning Professional
    Certified Building Commissioning Professional
    Certified Lighting Efficiency Professional
    Certified Measurement & Verification Professional
    Certified Power Quality Professional
    Certified Renewable Energy Professional
    Certified Building Energy Simulation Analyst
    Certified Green Building Engineer

National Council on Qualifications for the Lighting Professions

    Lighting Certified

Reputation Design+Build

American Academy of Environmental Engineers

> Board Certified Environmental Engineer
> Board Certified Environmental Engineering Member

Institute of Hazardous Materials Management

> Certified Hazardous Materials Practitioner
> Certified Hazardous Materials Manager

Project Management Institute

> Project Management Professional
> Program Management Professional
> PMI Risk Management Professional
> PMI Scheduling Professional
> Certified Associate in Project Management

Academy of Geo-Professionals

> Diplomate, Geotechnical Engineering

National Registry of Environmental Professionals

> Certified Environmental and Safety Compliance Officer
> Registered Environmental Manager
> Associate Environmental Professional
> Certified Environmental Auditor
> Registered Environmental Property Assessor
> Certified Environmental Systems Manager
> Certified Indoor Air Quality Manager
> Certified Environmental Scientist
> Certified Industrial Environmental Toxicologist
> Registered Hazardous and Chemical Materials Manager
> Registered Environmental Laboratory Technologist
> Registered Environmental Professional

Environmental Technician
Certified Refrigerant Compliance Manager
Certified Mold Inspector
Mold Awareness Specialist
Sustainability Initiatives Manager

BICSI

Registered Communications Distribution Designer

American Board of Industrial Hygiene

Certified Industrial Hygienist
Certified Associate Industrial Hygienist

Society for Marketing Professional Services

Certified Professional Services Marketer

Society for Human Resource Management

Professional in Human Resources
Senior Professional in Human Resources

Green Globes

Green Globes Professional
Green Globes Assessor

As you can see, there's a lot of professional associations serving the A/E/C industry. Fortunately, only a couple of all those listed actually apply to you.

The Tools:

- Professional Licensure (PE, RA, etc.)
- LEED AP or LEED Green Associate
- Professional Certifications: CCS, CDT, ICC
- Industry-Specific Certifications: ASHE
- Non-Technical Certifications: PHR, CPSM

Next Steps:

1. Determine industry expectations for someone with your desired brand, and analyze any gaps in licensure or certification; begin working towards that goal.

2. Review client RFPs and qualification requests to determine required credentials for specific project types.

3. Download relevant licensure/certification forms and begin preparing, even if you are not ready for the test/review process – this will further help identify gaps in knowledge and experience.

4. Research training opportunities – from professional societies, higher education providers, third-party corporations, online.

5. Attend review courses.

6. Investigate targeted CEU opportunities that will allow you to meet CEU requirements for existing licenses/certifications while gaining skills in an identified growth area or for future licensure or certification.

The Baseline: You're Only as Good as Your Portfolio

When the Federal Government replaced the outdated Standard Form 254/255 with the Standard Form 330, they served notice that the individual credentials of team members were a critical component of the A/E selection process. Gone were the days of relevant projects here, team members there. With the new form, design firms now had to demonstrate that the proposed team members had actually worked on the example projects.

The project experience of each individual team member has increasingly become a key evaluator when clients review design and construction teams. I used to have a simple rule that I called "3 in 3" or "5 in 5"; that is, three relevant projects completed in the past three years or five relevant projects completed in the past five years. But that rule was for *firm* experience, not for *individual* experience. Today, that simple rule can easily apply to every key project team member – project manager, architect, engineers, estimator, construction manager, project superintendent, etc. Your firm relies on your personal experience to help it get work.

Your portfolio is both a door opener and door closer. Part of your brand is based upon the projects you've been involved with. And it's not just the projects, it's also your role in those projects. If your goal is to position yourself as an expert in the planning of college campuses, you could specialize in the planning aspect (doer) or the management aspect (manager). Both are vital roles, but they must match your career path, your brand. If you are a planner but want to position yourself as an expert in managing the campus planning process, than you have a gap. You need to work toward becoming the project manager to build a portfolio that matches your desired brand. Is there any opportunity within your firm to gain that project management experience? Can you serve as an assistant project manager, gaining experience while providing value to your co-workers by going beyond your core position (planner)? Is there an opportunity to make the jump from planner to project manager by moving to another office within your firm or joining a different company altogether? How many projects does it take to qualify you as an "expert"? Three is a beginning. Five is better. A dozen or more should certainly put you there. But you can leverage a less-than-robust portfolio by using some other tools (e.g., write an article or blog featuring a case study of the one relevant project with which you were actively involved).

During an owner panel discussion at SMPS Build Business 2014, panelist John Perez of Cumming Corporation addressed the importance of personal experience: "A project executive in a recent proposal was really young. We did homework on the individual and learned that he was a superintendent only six months earlier. Don't do something like that – he clearly was not qualified for the project, so we eliminated his firm."

As you build your reputation, you may use those projects that directly relate to your field as expertise, as well as related or similar projects. Maybe you've never managed construction of a new hospital, but you've built several new medical clinics. That doesn't make you an expert at building hospitals, but does provide some relevant projects in your portfolio. If you truly want to focus on a type of project, it's incumbent upon you to do everything you can to position yourself to work on any of those types of projects, or related projects, that come through your firm. Or join a firm that does that kind of work – of course it's not as easy as picking up the phone and saying, "Hey, I want to manage hospital construction, and you build a lot of hospitals ... when can I start?" Rather, it requires a lot of research into firms that serve that market. Are they successful? Are they growing? Where can you meet and network with the people who make the hiring decisions? Are you passionate enough about the project type that you are willing to relocate just for an opportunity to become involved with the market segment? Or take a pay cut?

In the book *Outliers: The Story of Success*, author Malcolm Gladwell posits the "10,000-Hour Rule," essentially claiming that you should spend 10,000 hours doing a specific task to become an expert at it. That's roughly five years of your career devoted to one type of project or service to become an expert.

Awards are another component of your portfolio. First, there are the awards that your company wins, like an AIA or ABC award. You personally didn't win the award, but the overall project did; thus, as a member of the team, you are one of the owners of the award. Make sure any awards for projects in which you were involved are part of your portfolio. It's not bragging, just acknowledging your role in a successful project. Be sure to keep an eye out for potential award submissions – professional or technical organizations often have annual awards programs; magazines and industry publications frequently have awards programs as well. Offer to prepare the awards submission on behalf of your company or client. Be sure to also Google the project name occasionally – many times designers, contractors, and even developers submit the same project to separate awards programs but don't share information with one another. You may have worked on a project or two that won awards that you didn't know about!

Second are the individual-related awards, both industry and non-industry. *Building Design + Construction* has an annual Forty Under 40 awards program while *Engineering News-Record* has regional Top 20 Under 40 awards. These are national or regional in scope, and thus highly competitive. Your local business journal may also have a Forty Under 40 awards program. While still competitive – these awards are typically not limited to an industry or profession – you may have a greater chance of success with a program like this. What about the professional societies or technical organizations to which you belong? Many of them have awards programs, both at the chapter and national levels. What opportunities are there for you? For which awards do you qualify, and what is the nomination/submission process?

Fellowship in a professional association is also a type of award – recognition from your peers that you are a leader in the association and have done much to advance your profession. Most organizations award Fellow status to a very small percentage of members, so becoming a Fellow is a very prestigious honor – one that greatly enhances your brand and differentiates you from your colleagues and competitors.

You'll need to take some initiative here. Don't wait for an award to come to you – it probably won't happen. You may need to nominate yourself, or ask a colleague to nominate you. Don't be bashful – again, this is not about ego but about elevating your career and building your reputation. If a colleague agrees to submit a nomination on your behalf, prepare the application for them. Don't rely on them to prepare an award-winning application because only you know your unique value proposition and how it relates to the award. Be sure they know that you are giving them suggestions, and that they of course have free reign to make edits as they feel appropriate. And remember, they are doing you a huge favor, so ask how you can reciprocate. Be sure to send them a thank you note, at the minimum, or take them to lunch or give them a small gift or gift card.

Why should you care about awards? As it turns out, clients care about awards more than they used to. So do employers. Awards equal credibility. Design and construction awards reinforce your technical skills. Personal awards – whether industry-related or not – reinforce your brand as a leader and expert at something. Plus, with an increasing number of RFPs specifically asking for awards of the firm and awards of the team members, having a few awards on your resume is becoming an important component of marketing a company.

Photographs and renderings are actually another important component of your portfolio. We live in a visual society and we're all overloaded with information. A description of your past projects may *tell* about your experience, but it is often more important to *show* what you've done. Obtain as many photographs of projects you've been involved with as possible. Take them yourself, if you have to. Ask your firm's marketing department for electronic copies of photos they've obtained. If you are a designer, ask the contractor if they have any, or vice-versa. Electronic storage is cheap these days, so be liberal with your acquisition process. However, you must also be judicial with how you showcase them. No one needs to see 50 images of the same project. Two or three quality photographs of two or three projects relevant to your area of expertise may be all you need.

Three-dimensional models, computer renderings, animations and walk-throughs are all portfolio tools. So are complex schedules that you've developed, interesting diagrams and flowcharts, and anything else that visually reinforces your area of expertise and past experience.

A word of warning: be very cognizant of client confidentiality and ownership of copyrights. Your firm may have signed a non-disclosure agreement, and thus you are prohibited from sharing client information – including information from photographs and renderings. Likewise, copyright law protects the creator of the copyrighted work. Always get permission to use photos or drawings created by others (and if you photographed it or drew it while under the employ of a firm, the firm is the holder of the copyright – not you). Here's a tip: you can go photograph basically anything you want, as long as you are standing on public property like a street or sidewalk. If something is visible from a public place, it does not have any privacy protections (just check out your own home on Bing Maps or Google Earth). You can't necessarily feature it in an advertisement, which implies endorsement, but you can feature the images in your portfolio or on your website. That is, unless there is a nondisclosure agreement that prevents you – or your firm and its employees – from telling others that you were involved with a particular project or client.

So just how important is your portfolio?

Look no further than the U.S. General Services Administration's (GSA) Design Excellence Program. The submission requirements are fairly consistent for projects that are in this program. This particular example comes from a project solicitation for a new U.S. Courthouse in South Carolina. The building was budgeted to be in the $60 million to $70 million range, 200,000 square feet in size, and achieve LEED Gold certification.

From the Selection Process narrative:

> "This is a request for qualifications (RFQ) of A-E firms, and their associated lead designers, interested in contracting for this work. The A-E firm as used in this RFQ means an individual, firm, partnership, corporation, association, or other legal entity permitted by law to practice the profession of architecture or engineering that will have contractual responsibility for the project design. The lead designer is the individual or the team of designers who will have primary responsibility to develop the concept and the project design.
>
> "The A-E selection will be completed in two stages as follows: In Stage I, interested A-E firms, and their associated lead designers will submit portfolios of accomplishment that establish the design capabilities of the lead designer and A-E firm. In Stage II, shortlisted design teams, including all sub-consultants, will be assessed and representatives of the team interviewed."

Tools Part I: The Baseline

So here the GSA is making clear that the portfolio of the lead designer is the overriding factor in deciding which teams will advance to the second stage. They really aren't interested in the overall design team, just the lead designer, which is in this case an architect.

Later in the project solicitation, the GSA lists the Evaluation Criteria and Submission Requirements:

(1) Past Performance of the A-E Firm. This represents 35% of their scoring system, and requires:

> "The A-E firm(s) will submit a portfolio of not more than five projects completed in the last ten years (maximum of five pages per project). The narrative shall address the design approach with salient features for each project and discuss how the client's program, functional, image, mission, economic, schedule and operational objectives were satisfied by the overall design/planning solution. It should comment on the relevance of submitting projects to the GSA project, including features of sustainability, the urban design strategy, and workplace design. This section of the submission should include tangible evidence such as certificates, awards, peer recognition, etc., demonstrating design excellence, and provide a client reference contact for each project, including name, title, address, email, phone, and fax numbers. A representative floor plan, a site plan, and building section, or other appropriate drawing, and a minimum of two photographs must be included for each project."

This requirement is fairly typical on RFQs/RFPs, and actually gives some leeway in that they are allowing submitting firms to go back ten years, not just three or five. Here's where they ask for project awards. The next section focused on the lead designer:

(2) Lead Designer Portfolio. This represents 25% of the overall Stage I score, and requires:

"Submit a portfolio representative of the lead designer's ability to provide design excellence. Address his or her participation in each project. If a single designer, submit a portfolio of up to three projects completed in the last ten years (maximum of five pages per project). If the lead designer is a team, submit graphics and a description of up to two projects from each lead designer or lead design discipline. The narrative shall address the design philosophy with salient features for each project and discuss how the client's program, functional, image, mission, economic, schedule, and operations and maintenance objectives were satisfied by the overall design/planning solution. Include tangible evidence such as certificates, awards, peer recognition, etc., demonstrating design excellence. Where there is duplication with criteria (1) Past Performance on Design, the lead designer shall address his or her participation in the project."

With this requirement, the focus turns to the individual, or few individuals, who will be performing the lead architectural design. Again, the GSA wants photographs, graphics, awards, and other portfolio items. Next up is the lead designer's project approach:

(3) Philosophy and Design Intent, which represents another 25% of the scoring criteria.

"In the lead designer's words (maximum of two pages), as related to this project, state: the parameters of an overall design philosophy; his/her approach to the challenge of public architecture and related issues; parameters that may apply in creating a contemporary courthouse that is respectful of its context; and commitment to a high-level of integrated and sustainable design."

That's a lot to pack into two pages, but once again the GSA is focusing on the lead designer and how he or she proposes to approach the project. Finally, a biography of the lead designer:

(4) Lead Designer Profile, which represents the remaining 15% within the scoring system.

"Submit a biographical sketch (maximum of three pages) including education, professional experience, recognition for design efforts inclusive of the portfolio examples. Identify and describe areas of responsibility and commitment to each project."

The GSA Design Excellence Program really boils down to the brand of one or two key people. The title of this section of the book is "The Baseline," and the baseline for this program is the presence of a well-branded architect on the A/E team. All the tools featured in this section are essentially required as part of the Stage I submission: education, licenses, certifications, design awards, personal awards, specific project experience, related project experience, photographs, and graphics. Plus, the GSA is requiring a further demonstration of expertise from the lead designer(s) in the form of a narrative about their design philosophy and specific approach to the project. And this is all *before* they even want to see the entire project team. Only a branded architect – within a firm or head of their own practice – will meet the qualifications.

These types of requirements also appear in Requests For Proposals for construction services. In one example from a recent construction project, the solicitation required resumes for the proposed project executive, project manager, and general superintendent. These are the minimum requirements, as outlined in the RFP, and the overall scoring accounts for 25% of the decision process. The items in bold appeared that way in the RFP:

"**Project Executive**: The Project Executive for this contract shall be a principal (a person having authority) of the firm and shall have a minimum of **twenty (20) years** experience in new construction and/or renovation projects. A more favorable evaluation will be given to offerors who submit a Project Executive who exceeds these minimum requirements.

"**Project Manager**: The Project Manager for this contract shall have a **college degree** (bachelors of architecture, engineering, or construction management). The Project Manager shall possess a minimum of **twelve years** of project management experience and have managed two projects with a minimum cost of **$60,000,000**. The Project Manager should have experience with electronic project management (ePM) tools. A more favorable evaluation will be given to offerors who submit a Project Manager who exceeds these minimum requirements and has experience with ePM.

"**General Superintendent**: The General Superintendent shall have a minimum of **twelve years** of construction experience as a superintendent on **two projects** with a minimum cost of **$60,000,000**. The General Superintendent should have experience with electronic project management (ePM) tools. A more favorable evaluation will be given to offerors who submit a General Superintendent who exceeds these minimum requirements and has experience with ePM.

"In evaluating offers that exceed the minimums stated above, the following order of importance applies (most important to least): Project Manager, General Superintendent and Project Executive."

After reading these examples, do you now see how much your company needs your credentials to bring in work?

The Tools:

- Industry-specific project experience
- Industry-related project experience
- Project roles (e.g., project manager, designer, LEED administrator, estimator)
- Project awards
- Personal awards
- Project photographs
- Patents

Reputation Design+Build

Case Study: Carl Elefante, FAIA, LEED AP

"The greenest building is the one that is already built." These words, first uttered by architect Carl Elefante, are the rallying cry for green preservationists across the nation and beyond. Carl is a national expert on sustainable preservation and serves as Principal and Director of Sustainability with Quinn Evens Architects in Washington, DC. He also directs the firm's higher education efforts. Carl has been able to build an impressive portfolio of historic preservation projects that integrate sustainable design features. In the process, he has leveraged this experience into a long list of accomplishments that have built his brand as one of the nation's leading experts on the marriage between existing buildings and green buildings.

Based upon the strength of his portfolio, Carl has been able to present on the topic of sustainable preservation to such organizations as the American Institute of Architects, National Trust for Historic Preservation, Association for Preservation Technology International, US Green Building Council, Vancouver Heritage, Historic Districts Council of New York, National Building Museum, and US Department of Energy Office of Efficiency and Renewable Energy. He has served on President Clinton's Sustainable Communities Task Force, co-chaired APTI's Sustainable Preservation Technical Committee, and been a founding member of the National Capital Region Chapter of the US Green Building Council.

As Carl has steadily built his reputation on the national stage, his efforts have helped clarify the Quinn Evans brand, both internally and externally. The firm has created an external brand through working on such projects as the renovations of the National Academy of Sciences in Washington, DC and Robert S. Vance Federal Building and US Courthouse in Birmingham, Alabama, both of which had a very high level of green preservation. Internally, the company brand is two-fold: first, Quinn Evans is *the* existing building green architects; second, they have a broader commitment to sustainable stewardship.

Carl joined Quinn Evans in 1996 and brought with him the concept of "sustainable stewardship." In the late 1990s he became involved with the Dana Building on the campus of the University of Michigan. Quinn Evans worked with William McDonough + Partners on the landmark project, which had the benefit of providing Carl with a depth of understanding of green buildings while giving legitimacy to Quinn Evans in the field of sustainable preservation. According to Carl, "That's the building that really brought it all together. That's the poster child." The building won multiple awards from the AIA in both Michigan and Maryland. Another project that greatly impacted Carl was 71 Garfield Street in Detroit. A Historic Tax Credit project, Carl notes that it was a very important building to the surrounding African-American community, and became a symbol of "Detroit Rising." His firm liked the building so much that today they maintain an office in it. "When you can make an exciting place out of something that wasn't exciting, that's a real feel good story."

Next Steps:

1. Identify the target role (e.g., lead architect, specifier, project manager) and type of building/structure/project (e.g., laboratory, performing arts, bridge, historic) on which you want to focus.

2. Ask your supervisor, if applicable, to serve in the target role on the target building/structure/project.

3. If you have your own firm and are lacking credentials, look for teaming partners to pursue the type of work on which you want to focus – this will build your project portfolio.

4. Research and submit to awards programs projects that you and your firm designed or constructed.

5. Research and submit to awards programs that single you out as an individual; recruit a colleague to nominate you and ghostwrite the nomination if necessary.

Tools Part 2: Building Your Reputation

If the baseline is the price of admission, this next section is about everything else that you bring to the party. There are a lot of tools presented, and you may in fact be doing some of them already. As your read through this section, think about your own personal path of least resistance. Some of the tools will require you to step out of your comfort zone – or perhaps go far beyond it – and it just might not be realistic at this stage of your career. So focus on those tools that (1) you feel comfortable with, and (2) you think you can do well. If you are afraid of public speaking (one of the top American fears, by the way), you can *plan* to do it, but until you get over that fear, it is probably not a realistic goal to have.

One of the single easiest reputation-building tools that you can implement immediately is community involvement. Get engaged with a local business organization or non-profit in need. You may very well be a member of one or more professional associations, but how active are you? Do you sit on a committee or board?

Community and professional associations can be stepping stones to becoming involved with client organizations, which can greatly enhance your personal brand.

Writing for publication and public speaking are amazing brand-building tools for you and your firm. They also happen to be great business development tools, as owners increasingly look to the authors of articles in the publications they read, or speakers at the programs they attend, as potential candidates to work on their next projects. These tools also help build a large network, or can position you initially as a local or regional subject matter expert, and eventually a national expert at a particular topic of note.

Likewise, getting quoted by media is a powerful reputation-building tool because of the credibility that comes with it. Of course, you probably don't have a lot of reporters calling you right now for quotes, so you have to work to position yourself to become a source to media.

One of the newer reputation-building tools that wasn't readily available even a decade ago is social media, and many professionals have been able to greatly increase their personal brands and even enhance their careers by participating in various social media platforms. There are also a number of tools that you might not even think about as conduits for enhancing your reputation, like art and photography, coaching your child's sports team, or leading a Scout group. But these can also be powerful tools to make new connections and establish a positive name for yourself.

Ultimately, much of your reputation revolves around whom you know – your network. The challenge for all of us is to build our reputations among the people who we really want to receive our messages. A great personal brand in front of the wrong audience doesn't make much sense for them or us. Your network and the knowledge you are able to provide to it define you and can create a whole new world of opportunities. So once you've moved beyond

Tools Part 2: Building Your Reputation

the baseline tools of education, licenses/certifications, and experience, it's time to jump into the big leagues!

You Know Your Community – Do They Know You?

If there is a "low-hanging fruit" for reputation building, it is community involvement, sometimes referred to as "community trusteeship" or "servant leadership." Non-profit organizations need your skills, and they are lacking in volunteers. The United Way wants your money – and they want you to help them raise funds. Your local chamber of commerce wants you to be more active and attend their functions. There are a lot of opportunities near you, and sometimes all you need to do to get involved is just ask!

A good approach to becoming involved is to research whether or not your local community has a leadership training program, usually with a name like Leadership Philadelphia or Leadership Detroit. The length of the program varies from community to community – and some organizations have multiple programs of differing lengths – but their mission is common: train tomorrow's community leaders. Participants learn about the various needs of their community, and the non-profit organizations that work to fill those needs. Participants also receive training in how to lead and manage organizations, preparing them to serve on non-profit committees and boards of directors. Many of these programs offer a placement service upon graduation to match participants with their passions. These organizations provide a great way to get involved.

Does your firm belong to a chamber of commerce? Most do, even if no staff members actively participate. Chambers host networking events, trade shows, business training, and a multitude of other services for their members. You may be able to gain a few skills and build your network in the process. Beyond the chambers, your community may also have an economic development organization focused on recruiting new companies while maintaining existing ones. Once again, they offer various events for their members, and often have openings for board or committee members. Depending upon your brand focus, involvement with an organization like this may actually help you meet potential clients.

The United Way of America is one of the nation's top charities, and they are well-known to most people through their annual campaigns. Local United Way organizations serve as a fundraising arm for other local non-profits, but also provide expertise to those organizations through their Loaned Executive program. They need to cast a wide net for fundraising, so there are opportunities to serve in various industry cabinets. In fact, making a fundraising call for the United Way might actually provide a great excuse to meet someone that you want in your network. You can also volunteer on an allocations panel, reviewing the non-profit organization funding requests and recommending how much to distribute.

I've had the pleasure to serve on many committees and boards of directors for non-profit organizations, and I've personally gotten a lot out of my experiences. One of my passions is community service, so I think it is important for people in the business community to find an organization or two whose mission they really support, and volunteer. Economic development and community redevelopment – rebuilding our urban cores – strike a chord with me, so I've served on the boards of the local visitor's bureau, Main Street organization, and architectural preservation organization, serving as an officer for two of them. Use of this branding tool also led to opportunities to use other branding tools – I wrote and photographed seven visitors' guides and gave presentations to diverse groups on topics ranging from local history to architecture to green preservation. In the process, I met a lot of new people and expanded my network.

What community needs are you passionate about? Children's issues? The arts? The local economy? Health care? Education? There are many opportunities to become involved. I've never been involved with a non-profit organization that didn't want more volunteers, so if you are willing, these organizations are wanting. It is great for your reputation if you eventually become a leader of the organization by serving as a director or even an officer, but you don't have to start there. Volunteer at an organization's event. Join a committee and serve that way. A lot of non-profit work gets done at the committee level. You'll be raising your visibility and helping a cause that you are passionate about. What's the downside?

If you are worried about time commitment, you have a valid concern. So don't overextend yourself. I've found that I'm most effective when serving on two boards. When I add a third board of directors, something has to give. If you have your own company, it is fairly easy to say, "I'm going to commit x hours every month to serving the community." But if you work for a firm, it becomes more of a challenge. Most businesses are willing to allow their employees to serve non-profits, even if it means that they are away from the office during core work hours. Some companies require employees to make up the time (a bad business practice, by the way) while others see the benefits of having their employees engaged in the local community.

Not only is community service an important tool in building your reputation, but it also positively reflects your company's brand. Businesses do business with like-minded firms. In fact, I can think of several projects that my company was awarded that had a direct tie to the community service of staff. In some cases, a lead came through this channel. In other cases, the client actually used community involvement as an evaluation criterion. And when you compete against that "out-of-town expert," the fact that you and your firm are committed to the local community can be leveraged as a key differentiator.

There's another benefit of community service: recruiting. Study after study has indicated that the Millennial generation is passionate about making a difference. They want to feel that what they do matters. So they are interested in working for companies that de-

Tools Part 2: Building Your Reputation

sign and construct projects that help others. But they also want to be involved themselves. They want to know that their supervisors and co-workers are actively helping to better their communities. In fact, many Millennials expect this behavior, and some won't work for a firm that doesn't embrace it. With the impending A/E/C workforce shortage, it is critical for companies to be active in the communities they serve – and thus your role in the community will become increasingly important for recruiting and maintaining employees.

An extension of community service is becoming involved with institutions. For many professionals, this means being involved with their college alumni organization. For others, it means serving on advisory committees or boards of trustees for their local educational institutions – public schools, charter schools, community colleges, technical schools, private colleges and universities. Is there any opportunity for you to become involved, starting with any organization tied to your college and your major? Maybe there is a health care institution in your community with advisory committees and a board of trustees.

One of the reasons I often hear for people not getting involved is, "I can't afford to." There is a perception that serving on nonprofit boards and organizations requires a substantial outlay of cash. There will be an expense, but it may be limited to an annual fee to join the organization and maintain your membership, particularly if you are an event volunteer or committee member. At the board level, there is an expectation that you contribute to fundraising campaigns. With a few organizations, this number may be significant. But with most organizations, it may be as little as $100 or $200, and even less in many cases.

With all the organizations I've been involved with, I've learned that there seems to be a pretty consistent breakdown between board members. One-third are the "funders." They are typically older, and are major financial contributors to the organization.

They may actually be inactive board members. The second third are the "doers." This is where I typically fall. The doers work hard to make sure the business of the organization is moving forward and the mission is being met. Non-profit organizations usually don't have nearly enough staff members, so the doers often function as adjunct staff. Finally, there are the "do-nothings," which represent the remaining third of the board. The do-nothings don't contribute much money – the staff may have to regularly remind them to renew their membership. They also do little, if any, work to support the organization. They may go many months between attending board meetings. Sometimes they simply view their board position as a line-item on their resume. Other times they are simply far too overextended. The problem is that they give off negative energy, and tend to pull the other board members down. They also are the ones that complain or disagree at the few meetings they actually do attend.

Aspire to be a funder one day, but for now focus on being a doer. And when you are an effective doer, word gets around and other organizations began contacting you to see if you are interested in joining their committees and boards, too.

The Tools:

- Leadership *Yourtown*
- Chamber of Commerce
- United Way
- Non-Profit Organizations
- Educational/Health Care Institutions

Tools Part 2: Building Your Reputation

Case Study: John Klinedinst, PE

John Klinedinst is president and CEO of C.S. Davidson, Inc., a 75-person civil and municipal engineering firm located in York, Pennsylvania. In addition to the firm's headquarters office, C.S. Davidson maintains two regional offices. Their business model is built around becoming the go-to firm in the areas they serve, and being active in their communities is part of their corporate core values. No one exemplifies this more than John, who is a sought-after member of the local business and non-profit communities.

He has served on the boards of directors for many organizations, often as an officer or president at some time during his tenure. John has served as president of the Rotary Club of York, president of the Sertoma Club of York, chair of the York County Chamber of Commerce, trustee of Yorkshire United Methodist Church, and director of the following organizations: Cultural Alliance of York County, Crispus Attucks York, Penn State York Advisory Council, YWCA of York, and York County Economic Alliance, to name a few. He has been the York County Chamber of Commerce Volunteer of the Year, Downtown Inc (Main Street affiliated organization) Outstanding Volunteer, *Central Penn Business Journal* Outstanding Executive of the Year Finalist, and received the Sertoma Lifetime Achievement Award plus a Rotary International Paul Harris Fellow. All of this is in addition to being the president of a successful engineering firm.

John sums up his belief about community trusteeship: "Involvement by professionals in the community through service on boards of nonprofits is recognized by the business community as an asset, an investment back to the community. That helps promote the business vision that while projects and clients are important, and they are, it isn't all about work; it is about being a part of the community." And while involvement in the community has built a very positive reputation, he believes that, "It's not so much about the reputation, it is about community service by interested businesses."

John doesn't believe that community service by itself is a direct source of work for his firm, but rather it is about even more than that: "For the company, and my representation as the company president, it's not about getting work; it's about being part of the community – it is one of our fundamental core values. I've personally had extraordinary opportunities through my community work to meet people and do things I never would do ordinarily: from interviews on radio and TV to print about projects or events or positions, to tours of facilities most people don't get to see, to meeting elected officials and really getting to discuss issues with them, it has been rewarding." John's investment in the community, as well as the time spent by those who work with him, has greatly increased the firm's exposure. Additionally, he says: "I've gotten more out of my community service than I put into it, and I believe that I've grown as a person, executive, and member of the community as a result."

Next Steps:

1. Research potential community and service organizations that align with your passions.
2. Determine the "best fit" or two.
3. Reach out to those organizations and inquire about becoming involved at the committee or board level.
4. Obtain event information and attend a few events to get a feel for the organization and their purpose or mission.
5. Be liberal with your follow-up activities after events/meetings – notes, thank you letters, inputting contacts into your CRM database.

Tools Part 2: Building Your Reputation

Most communities have dozens or even hundreds of non-profit organizations in need of volunteers to serve on local/chapter boards of directors and committees or to participate in events. Some of the major national organizations with local offices throughout the country include:

- American Cancer Society
- American Red Cross
- Boy Scouts of America
- Boys & Girls Club of America
- Catholic Charities USA
- Girl Scouts of America
- Goodwill Industries International
- Habitat for Humanity International
- March of Dimes
- National Main Street Center
- National Trust for Historic Preservation
- The Arc of the United States
- The Salvation Army
- United Way of America
- YMCA of the USA
- YWCA USA

Leading Your Peers Through Professional Associations

If community service is the low-hanging fruit of reputation-building tools, professional association involvement is on the branches immediately above. The terminology commonly used for this tool includes professional organizations and technical societies. Some people use "professional" to signify only organizations comprising licensed professionals and "technical" to reference societies with non-licensed professionals. To me that's just splitting hairs, so we'll lump everything together here, with one important clarification. These are not societies for specific market sectors or owner groups (those organizations appear in the next section and are referred to as client organizations). So groups of builders, subcontractors, construction managers, engineers, environmental scientists, architects, interior designers, etc., all fall within this category.

These organizations directly relate to what you do for a living, so if you're a civil engineer your professional associations may include the American Society of Civil Engineers and American Consulting Engineers Council. If you work for a construction firm, your professional associations may include Associated Builders & Contractors and the Society of Cost Estimating and Analysis. While these organizations may include clients or prospective clients, particularly if you are a subconsultant or subcontractor, they are primarily focused on elevating the profession or practice through education and advocacy. Many also hold annual conferences and offer certification programs. Furthermore, most of these associations have regional or local chapters, providing great opportunities to get involved.

Involvement is the key word here. Professional associations have many members who have absolutely no involvement other than paying their annual dues. The American Institute of Architects

(AIA) is a voluntary organization – architects do not have to join. To practice and seal drawings, architects take a licensure exam to become Registered Architects (RA). And for a lot of them, that is enough. But membership in the AIA is viewed by many as more prestigious; in fact, thousands of architects use AIA behind their name instead of RA. One who uses AIA is an RA with professional membership in the AIA. But a lot of architects go no further than paying their annual membership dues and completing required continuing education. To them, the only important thing is the ability to use AIA behind their name as a differentiator.

For other architects, though, participation in AIA – through their local or state chapter, or the national organization – is a means of giving back to the profession. They join committees and boards, mentor intern architects, advocate for the profession, attend lectures and conferences, and maybe even go to the National Convention to learn about new products, design techniques, and industry trends. Through the process, they regularly network with their peers. Some may be colleagues or former co-workers; others may be future employers or employees.

These are the primary benefits of being active in your professional association: education, advocacy, networking. Sometimes, these organizations even become support groups. Things that may frustrate you about the profession – or your company or co-workers – probably also frustrate other people in your shoes, so it is nice to talk through the challenges you face with others in similar situations.

There is another important benefit about becoming active in your professional association: it differentiates you from others. Clients see it on your resumes: John is a licensed Professional Engineer and has been an environmental engineer for 20 years; Jane is a licensed Professional Engineer and Board Certified Environmental Engineer and has been an environmental engineer for 14 years, but she has also served as State Representative to the American Academy of Environmental Engineers and on the board of directors for her local chapter of the National Society of Professional Engineers. John is a doer. Jane is a leader. That is the message that comes across to clients, and potential employers, while reviewing John's and Jane's credentials.

Where should you begin? The first – and most obvious – step in the process is to actually *join* the professional associations related to your experience and expertise. There may be several options, and you may already belong to one or two professional associations.

Just like with community involvement, the opportunities for you to build your reputation with professional association involvement may be close by. Are there local or regional chapters of these organizations? If so, begin attending the meetings if you aren't already doing so. Just being there will help you build your network and can advance your knowledge base on a particular topic.

But don't just attend, become active. Volunteer to serve on a committee (hint: program and sponsorship committees are always looking for fresh blood!) and don't just participate at meetings, but work to advance the committee between meetings. Nominate yourself to serve on the board of directors, or ask a colleague to nominate you. Be sure the current president and vice president are aware of your interest, because if you are an active doer, they may pull a few strings to get you on their board.

Leadership in these associations can further advance your brand. It demonstrates to your employer that you have leadership and management skills. It demonstrates to your colleagues that you are dedicated to advancing your profession. It demonstrates to clients, prospects, and future employers that you are a leader in your profession, not a follower.

Another great way to maximize your involvement with these organizations is through attending conferences, as well as writing articles for their newsletters or magazines and speaking at local, regional, and national meetings and conferences. These are all excellent tools to enhance your reputation and expand your network.

Early in my career, I stumbled across the Society for Marketing Professional Services, an association comprising marketing and business development professionals from the A/E/C industry. Being located in a mid-market area, there wasn't a local chapter. So I began attending meetings of the Baltimore chapter – about an hour away, and Philadelphia chapter – approximately two hours away. Then one day representatives from the Philadelphia chapter came to central Pennsylvania and said that the area fell under their territory, and they really thought that an affiliate chapter could work. As I had gotten to know a few colleagues from central Pennsylvania who also made regular trips to Philadelphia, I offered to help them create a new chapter. SMPS Central Pennsylvania was born – under the umbrella of SMPS Philadelphia. Over the next several years I served on the governing committee (essentially acting as a board of directors) as membership chair, sponsorship chair, and secretary. Because we were affiliated with the Philadelphia chapter, my network expanded and I was recruited to join their program committee and eventually became newsletter editor for a few years.

With roughly two million people, central Pennsylvania is a pretty vibrant and growing area – one that was ripe for a new chapter. Although it was affiliated with Philadelphia during my six years on the governing committee, it has since become an independent chapter. This story has two morals. First, if there is a need, fill it. If there isn't a local chapter, maybe there is one within an hour of you. Or, maybe there is a need for a local chapter to be established – take the initiative! Second, don't go it alone – there are certainly other talented people in your profession, located nearby, who could work with you to create something special.

And remember, just because one organization doesn't have a local chapter, there may be a few other potential associations that do have something nearby. If you don't already know, a few minutes on the Internet should answer your questions.

I'm such a big fan of professional associations, but do confess to a bit of frustration when I hear people say, "There's nothing in it for me." Of course there is – but like everything else, you get out of it what you put into it. Part of the disconnect is narrow thinking. I've worked with some engineers who simply thought that they knew more than enough about their discipline, so that their professional association couldn't provide any value. Yet it is their association that advocates for the advancement of their profession. There's value. They could be expanding their network – because today's competitors are tomorrow's teammates. More value. They could be meeting young engineers that would be a perfect fit for their company – or potential future employers. Value and value. If they served on committees or the board, they would be learning new leadership and management skills – managing an organization is different than managing a project. They could position themselves to become a leader in their firm. Additional value. They would be forced into an environment where they had to smile and be friendly and meet new people – an important skill as they work to build their network. Additional value. They could be calling owners and asking them to participate on panel discussions – indirectly making business development contacts. More value. They could be speaking in front of an audience at meetings – either welcoming the group, making announcements, moderating a panel, or giving a presentation. Enhanced speaking skills + comfort in front of an audience = yet more value. And finally, they could be writing newsletter articles, sponsorship letters, white papers, and more, getting their name out and once again gaining value from organizational participation.

Are you convinced yet? Your professional association is waiting – go be a leader! Check out Appendix A for a listing of potential organizations to join.

Tools Part 2: Building Your Reputation

The Tools:

- National professional associations related to your core expertise
- Regional and local chapters of those associations
- Specialized regional organizations
- Regular meeting attendance
- Committee and board service
- Regional and national conference attendance

Case Study: Judith Nitsch, PE, LEED AP BD+C

Judy Nitsch has achieved a level of success in professional associations that few design professionals could ever hope to accomplish. She is founder and chairwoman of Nitsch Engineering, an 80-person WBE civil and transportation engineering and land surveying firm. She is licensed in nineteen states and received an honorary Doctor of Science degree from the Massachusetts Maritime Academy in 2010. Her business practice is built upon both a deep dedication to industry organizations as well as a profound willingness to share information with anyone and everyone. She will tell you that a competitor today could be a client tomorrow.

Her impressive resume includes stints as president of the American Council of Engineering Companies of Massachusetts and the Boston Society of Civil Engineers Section/ASCE. She is recipient of the American Society of Civil Engineers' Parcel-Sverdrup Engineering Management Award, Boston Society of Architects Women in Design Award, Society of Women Engineers Entrepreneur Award, Woman of the Year recognition from the Women's Transportation Seminar – Boston Chapter, and Massachusetts Society of Professional Engineers' Young Engineer Award. But that is only the beginning of her credentials, as Judy has served on the Worcester Polytechnic Institute Board of Trustees, Board of the Greater Boston Chamber of Commerce, and as a Trustee of Eastern Bank. Her commitment to her profession has resulted in no less than four fellowships: Fellow of the American Council of Engineering Companies (ACEC), Fellow of the American Society of Civil Engineers (ASCE), Fellow of the Society of Women Engineers (SWE), and Fellow of the Society for Marketing Professional Services (SMPS).

"I grew up in a family where my parents were both involved in the community and our church, so when I graduated from college and started working, I thought getting involved was 'normal'," states Judy. She initially joined the Boston Society of Civil Engi-

Tools Part 2: Building Your Reputation

neers Section of ASCE and was recruited to serve on a committee working to plan a society convention that was scheduled to be held in Boston. "I didn't realize that I would be the youngest person and the only woman engineer on that committee! But I quickly realized that my role there gave me exposure to the senior civil engineers in Boston ... and I also realized that, as the only woman there, I really stood out to them!" An early lesson learned was that by becoming involved, volunteering, and doing what she said she'd do, Judy was able to create an environment in which her peers continued to want to work with her. As her career blossomed, Judy became involved with a number of organizations where she could interact with potential clients, including the Society for Marketing Professional Services, American Council of Engineering Companies, American Institute of Architects, and American Society of Landscape Architects. She says that, "The opportunity to get to know potential clients while working on a committee with them was priceless."

Today, the staff of Nitsch Engineering embraces the ideals of their founder. More than seventy percent of staff are active in at least one professional organization, with approximately one quarter of them serving in some form of leadership capacity. Overall, Nitsch Engineering staff participates in forty professional associations. For Judy, she's been able to raise her personal brand and gain national recognition. She credits involvement with the Society for Marketing Professional Services with helping take her career to new places. She originally became involved with the organization because she could meet marketing staff from potential clients. However, she states, "I also learned a lot about how to do business development, be better at client relations, and hone our marketing skills through SMPS. After that, I started looking for speaking opportunities at national venues like AIA, ASLA, SCUP, and GreenBuild ... all of which helped build our brand as an innovative civil engineering firm AND helped me get closer to important clients since I often asked them to be on a panel with me."

Next Steps:

1. Research professional associations that cover your area of expertise.
2. Determine which organizations offer the best "fit" for your passions as well as the greatest opportunity to expand your network and build your reputation.
3. Obtain meeting and event information, and then attend to get a feel for the organization's mission, purpose, and membership.
4. Join those associations that offer the greatest interest and opportunity.
5. Contact the organizations about committee and board openings and volunteer to serve.
6. Be liberal with follow-up after meetings and events – notes, thank-you letters, inputting contacts into your CRM database.

Client Organizations: Making Your Prospects Want to Meet You

Business developers view client organizations as the holy grail of networking. Whereas participation in community groups may help foster relationships with a few key local decision-makers, and involvement in professional associations may lead to new teaming partners (or sub-consulting and sub-contracting commissions), active membership in client organizations can put you in regular direct contact with decision-makers in the industries you target.

That's why a lot of A/E/C firms are involved with the International Facilities Management Association (IFMA), Association of Facilities Engineers (AFE), Construction Owners Association of America (COAA), and APPA (formerly known as the Association of Physical Plant Administrators), among others.

However, there is a fine line to walk in these organizations – you still need to provide value to the other members, and cannot ever come across as a leech that is only there to sell, sell, sell. Doing so is a sure-fire way to cause major damage to your reputation.

Don't join a client organization simply because you want to promote your company to the members. Join a client organization because you want to gain knowledge about the issues facing your clients, because you believe in the mission of the organization and will work to advance it, and because you are genuinely interested in developing relationships with other members of the organization.

Sometimes membership in these organizations falls under a category known as "affiliate," and there may be restrictions on how you can participate.

From the company level, it is important to exhibit at the organization's shows, advertise in the organization's newsletter, and sponsor the organization's meetings and events. These opportunities offer high visibility for your firm; however, the rubber really meets the road in the form of relationships. You can't rely on your company spending money but not personally getting involved.

If you want to build your reputation as an expert in a certain industry, active involvement in the related client organization is one way to elevate your credentials. As with other associations and societies, these organizations typically have local or regional chapters run entirely by volunteers. The chapter may have a board as well as several committees. Once you join an organization, find out where their needs are and volunteer to get involved. Participation on the membership committee offers a great way to meet new people and get your name in front of the chapter's members through renewal letters, building your name recognition. Involvement on the program committee allows you to have some input, and even control, into the content and speakers at meetings. Serving on the sponsorship committee helps raise your visibility because you'll be out there, representing the client organization, and trying to raise funds for it. In the process of committee service, you'll also find that you are developing relationships with other committee members, and soon you'll be in regular contact with them between organizational meetings.

Through these types of activities you'll build a positive reputation as someone who is proactively helping the organization, and thus the members, instead of someone who is carpet bagging for work. Good things will follow – maybe in the form of a request to author an article for the chapter newsletter, or to speak at a forthcoming program. One reputation-building tool can lead to another, and soon the client members will seek you out. Perhaps it will come in the form of a simple request to pick your brain or a more formal invitation to their office to introduce your company's credentials or to present an educational lunch-n-learn to their staff.

All this time you are not selling anything; rather, you are developing and then strengthening relationships with key people. You are using the client organization as a platform for building your own reputation, even while helping to build the brand of your firm.

The Tools:

- o   Industry-Focused Organizations (e.g., ASHE, APPA)
- o   Owner-Focused Organizations (e.g., COAA, IFMA, SCUP)

Reputation Design+Build

Case Study: William Johnson, CFM

William Johnson's background is in civil engineering, followed by a stint as a facility manager. Today he is client development manager at Terracon Consultants Inc., an environmental and geotechnical engineering firm. Although he has a technical background and is a Certified Facilities Manager, Bill's primary focus is business development. And while you might think that his focus would be "downstream" – doing business development with architects or civil engineers, for instance – he is actually on the front lines working directly with owners, particularly in the higher education market. Bill currently serves on the board of Second Nature and in the past has served on the boards of directors of Plan NH, John Stark Regional High School, and Leadership New Hampshire. He has even authored a book, *Business Development for Professionals*.

Bill is where his clients are and is involved with the International Facilities Management Association, APPA and ERAPPA – which are both related to higher education facilities management, Society for College and University Planning (SCUP), and the Association for Advancement of Sustainability in Higher Education (AASHE). He is recipient of the APPA Eagle and Rising Star Awards, a board member of AASHE, a Facilities Planning Academy Member of SCUP, and is also active in the Urban Land Institute (ULI) and Society for Marketing Professional Services (SMPS). Bill has authored articles for APPA's *Facilities Manager* magazine and moderated a webinar for the organization.

Why has Bill been so active with these client organizations? The answer is simple, according to him: "Involvement with these organizations increased my visibility and ability to get myself and my firm engaged. People want to know that you care." He's actually demonstrated this first-hand by helping his firm's clients sell internally to their own organizations: "I've had the opportunity to put together a fairly detailed and involved internal sales training program for facilities managers, basically teaching them how to sell internal to their own organizations." Bill has given this presentation in association with a university facilities director, and the responses have been overwhelmingly positive. So how did this opportunity come about? "This was an outgrowth of a conversation with the Executive Vice President of APPA and the then-chair of the board of directors over dinner. This wouldn't have happened if I didn't have relationships with them and hadn't already become a trusted source of information."

In his book *Business Development for Professionals*, Bill characterizes this client-level involvement as "Invading Organizations," and boils his advice down to four basic points: "Show up. Offer to help. Get involved. Reap the benefits."

Next Steps:

1. Research client organizations that fit with (1) your personal career goals, and (2) your company's strategic plan goals.
2. Obtain membership and event information.
3. Attend a few events to get a feel for their organization, including their mission and membership.
4. If appropriate, join one or more organizations.
5. Contact the organizations about opportunities for committee and board service.
6. Be judicial with follow-up, including notes, thank-you letters, and inputting contact information into your CRM database.
7. Support the organizations through advertising in their newsletter or magazine, participating in their trade shows, contributing articles, speaking at events, and being a valuable source of information to members.

Writing to Build Credibility

Writing is an excellent way to establish your reputation as a thought leader and reach a wide audience. But often there are a series of steps to go through, each one leading you to a larger audience and greater name recognition.

Before you can write a word, however, you first need a topic. What can you write about? Your topic will depend largely upon your audience. If your company publishes a newsletter or blog, you might write about a recent project experience with which you were involved. Don't just write about the end-result, though. If you only provide a data-dump of facts, you'll just be acting like a reporter from outside of the industry – and a boring one at that.

What was the client's project goal? Why did they embark on the project to begin with – was it to fill a need or better serve their clients or customers? What challenges were faced along the way, and how did you solve them? Did the project program change as a result of the challenges?

Every project needs a solution. Every project faces challenges. Design and construction professionals, however, often don't see what they do as anything special and don't view themselves as being any different from others in their industry. So you'll need to recognize your own brilliance! That is, when did you go "off script" through the course of a project? What did you, or your team, do that was atypical or innovative? Did your client expect miracles? What did you learn along the way?

These are stories, and interesting ones at that.

When used in company newsletters, these stories demonstrate your creativity and problem-solving skills to your clients, and also provide a way to share knowledge with other employees who may not have worked on the particular project.

Of course, writing about client experiences are just the tip of the iceberg when it comes to potential topics. (And there are always those pesky non-disclosure agreements to contend with.) Maybe you've been trying a new approach to programming, have figured out new ways to incorporate sustainability into a construction project, have utilized a totally different approach to the project management process, or have developed a totally new or innovative approach to prefabrication.

Branding is about distinction, so when you write it is important to cover topics that have not already been featured ad nauseam. You build your reputation by differentiating yourself, and an excellent way to do that is with knowledge sharing.

When you move beyond a very amenable publisher – you or your company – and into A/E/C or client-industry publications, you really need to have different content. Some publications employ full-time writers/reporters, and don't accept articles from outside sources. However, the majority of the magazines out there have small staffs and rely on outside sources for content. And while they are always hungry for new, interesting articles, they are also discerning when it comes to what they publish.

The topics must fit the purpose of their magazine and relate directly to their readers. If the magazine appeals to the automotive industry, your excellent case study of an institutional project is not going to interest them. If it is a publication targeting architects, an article about how a particular type of engineering system integrates with architecture may be acceptable, but an article that is *only* about the engineering system probably won't be.

It is not easy to get articles published in trade and industry publications, but you can enhance your odds of success by following their rules. First, read their magazine. Who are the article authors? Are they all staff writers, or are they professionals from the A/E/C or other industries? In the case of the former, there's limited – if any – opportunity for you to have your article published there. In the case of the latter, however, that's a pretty big clue that they accept articles from outside sources. Check out their website and see if you can find any "writer's guidelines" or "article submission guidelines." These will give you their "rules" – topics that they accept, recommended length of articles, contact person, and more. A publication that targets the A/E/C industry and accepts articles from outside writers is an easier road to travel than most client publications, which may only occasionally publish an article related to design or construction.

Professional associations and client organizations often publish newsletters or magazines. The content for these publications is often member-driven, so they may represent the greatest chance of success for you. First, start local. Does your local chapter publish a newsletter? There's probably a volunteer editor, and I can almost guarantee that he or she constantly struggles to have enough content. Contact them and offer to write an article. Discuss potential topics – what are they looking for, and what do you feel comfortable writing about? Most of the local chapter-based newsletters have shorter articles, often 500 words or less, so it won't require a major commitment of your time and you'll be helping out the organization. Actually, this is a great tool for expanding your network and laying the groundwork to potentially serve on a committee or the chapter's board of directors.

Some associations also have regional or state chapters. If they have publications, it is probably a bit more competitive for article placement, but still easier than with national association publications. Again, you have to reach out. While you could write an article and submit it for publication, your odds will be better if you first communicate with the editor to discuss potential topics. Understand that when they provide suggestions, they are not committing to publish whatever you submit, but they are helping you increase your chance of publication.

The nationally-focused (or internationally-focused) association publications are the most competitive to get into; however, these organizations may have a monthly or quarterly magazine, weekly newsletter, and blog or online e-zine. In other words, they may have several outlets requiring content. Get familiar with their various publications. Read the content. Who is writing it? Staff writers, association members, or perhaps a third-party content provider? Maybe a combination of all of these. If they don't have article submission guidelines on their website, or in the publication, reach out to the managing editor. Contact him or her. Ask if they accept articles from members. Request a copy of their writer's guidelines.

If they don't accept articles from non-staff, don't fret. There are so many print and digital publications out there, just move on to the next opportunity.

Also, don't overlook local publications. Is there a topic that ties your expertise to something that is happening locally? If so, perhaps you could write a letter to the editor of your local business journal or publication. Or find out who covers real estate, design, and construction. With a local newspaper, that may be the business editor. For a regional business journal, there may be a reporter specifically dedicated to this segment. A/E/C firms spend a lot to advertise in business journals, so the publications regularly feature content related to design and construction.

Most business journals have reporters that do the writing, but there may be occasional opportunities to submit an article with your byline, and certainly you can submit a letter to the editor. Furthermore, by reaching out to the reporter, you will also have the opportunity to provide information about your particular area of expertise and offer to assist the reporter in any way you can. You'll find more on this in the Making News section, but the goal here is to get your name in print. Even if you aren't the author, there's credibility associated with being quoted in the media.

No matter what you write, or where it is published, it needs to be written *well*. As covered in the first tool – You – the way you write says a lot about who you are. I've met a lot of design professionals who truly believe they are talented writers, yet the reality was far from their perception. Everyone needs an editor. And even if the publication has an editor, don't assume they will fix all your mistakes! They may look at a poorly-written article and decline to publish it because it is too unprofessional or because it will take too much of their time to edit and correct. If your firm has a marketing department, you probably have an editor on staff. That person will happily work with you to write the article, focus the message, and create crisp prose that will be greatly appreciated by the publication. If you don't have such a co-worker, you may need to reach out to your network – personal and professional. Do you know any English teachers? Do you have any colleagues who have been published? You may need to hire someone to edit your work – it's usually not that expensive, and it will pay positive dividends – but most likely you are already connected with someone who has editing skills. It is okay to ask them for a favor, as long as you offer to reciprocate and share your expertise with them. Be sure to send them a personalized thank you note, or food, or tickets to a sporting event, etc. No matter what, do not skip this step. You may be an excellent writer, but authors tend to read what they *meant* to write, not necessarily what they actually wrote. It takes another pair of eyes to catch certain errors and point out concepts that are potentially confusing to readers.

Also, whenever you write something, be thinking about how you can repurpose content. A blog post that you write for your company may also be used in the newsletter of a local professional association. An article written for a company newsletter could be repurposed, and possibly expanded, for a trade journal.

The first articles I ever wrote were for my company newsletter. Not being a technical person, I'd interview my engineer co-workers, conduct additional research, and write articles. I was essentially acting like a reporter. Then, I learned that a local newspaper was publishing a special supplement in association with the annual Engineers Week, and they were looking for articles. I contacted them and shared several company newsletters, and they then selected two articles for publication. The first time you see your byline in print it is quite exciting (and for me, addicting). Shortly thereafter, I happened to be reading over *The Military Engineer*, the magazine of the Society of American Military Engineers (SAME), and saw a call for articles related to a special energy issue that they had planned. My company had been doing some pretty cool stuff with thermal storage, and this had been one of the topics of a company newsletter, so I contacted the magazine editor and pitched the topic. He liked it, but informed me that the article had to be more substantial. I expanded upon what I had already written and submitted the article, which was accepted and published. In the process, I included quotes from the project manager, who was also a company executive, and helped build his reputation, too.

There are three lessons here. The first is that the content – the topic or idea – can be published and republished in multiple forms at multiple lengths. The second is that it is okay to go beyond your personal area of expertise (believe me, I know very little about thermal ice storage systems) if you approach your role as that of a reporter – researching the background, interviewing those knowledgeable about the topic. The third lesson is to start small and work your way up to larger publications. My first articles appeared in a company newsletter, and then reappeared in a newspaper supplement. And then I expanded one of the articles and it appeared in a magazine published by a client organization. This happened long before the appearance of weblogs (blogs), but if I were starting today, my initial foray into writing and publishing may very well be targeting professional and client associations with blogs.

Once you have several articles in your writing portfolio, you may want to consider moving to the next level. Articles help build your reputation, but white papers and books really take it to another level. The reason for this is that it takes a lot of research and time to author a white paper or book. Because of this, so few people actually do it. It takes a major commitment, and a lot of people simply aren't prepared to give that much of their time. But for those who do it, the reputation-building results are immense.

A white paper can be something that your company publishes, or something distributed through a professional association. And while a white paper makes a logical stepping stone between articles and books, there is still a substantial commitment involved. Wikipedia defines white paper as "an authoritative report or guide that helps solve a problem." The significant word here is authoritative. Readers expect to learn something that will help them. Today "white paper" has become somewhat of a generic term because so many companies post free white papers on their website – all you have to do is register to receive it, then they will gladly email you a PDF that demonstrates a problem and how it can only be solved if you purchase their product. White papers are gaining an undeserved bad reputation. Therefore, if you author one, make sure that it is research-based, with plenty of examples, and it actually provides value to the readers. By publishing through an association, your white paper will have a higher level of credibility.

More than eighty percent of Americans believe that they "have a book in them" according to a study published a few years ago. But it is a lot of work with little financial reward. Seth Godin, a best-selling business author, points this out on his blog: "The return on equity and return on time for authors and for publishers is horrendous. If you're doing it for the money, you're going to be disappointed. On the other hand, a book gives you leverage to spread an idea and a brand far and wide. There's a worldview that's quite common that says that people who write books know what they are talking about and that a book confers some sort of authority."

If you write a book, you should do so because (1) you enjoy the process or challenge, and (2) you have something to say. There are a lot of books out there missing readers. Actually, most books are missing readers. Some industry research that I've come across has found that eighty percent of books from traditional publishers (not self-published) sell less than 99 copies in a given year. Think about that – you spend 700 hours, or more, writing a book, and less than one hundred people actually read it! Only four percent of books sold in the U.S. sell more than 1,000 copies. And most of those books are sold by "brand name" authors. Plus, as Godin mentioned, the ROI is horrible. In fact, you'll most certainly work for less than minimum wage.

But what you get in return is reputation as a thought-leader. As an innovator. As an expert. Today's publishing options are myriad. The odds of a major publisher picking up your work are incredibly small, but there may be an opportunity with a niche publisher or A/E/C-related publisher. You can self-publish (check out Amazon's CreateSpace service) or create an ebook, either in PDF format or on Amazon's Kindle.

Have you ever downloaded an excellent ebook for free and thought, "Why is the author giving it away?" The answer is they know that there is so little money in book writing, so by giving it away for free they are hoping to reach the broadest audience possible.

Keep in mind, when writing blogs, articles, or books, you need to think big-picture. If you are an estimator, don't limit yourself to estimating-related topics. Are there broader construction issues that you've experienced? Are there six errors that you consistently find on A/E drawings? Do you have any hobbies that you are really good at?

I'm not an architect, but I'm really interested in historic buildings. I've written a couple of books specifically about historic architecture. One was about the historic buildings in my community, and another was about the architectural styles in the region in which I live. I'm qualified to write about these topics because I've done the research. Extensive research, in fact, over the period of more than a decade. I'm qualified to write a book about reputation management in the design and construction industry because I've been part of this industry for more than twenty years; I've seen first-hand how important personal brands are becoming; I've read numerous books and blogs and articles on the topic; I've conducted several online surveys to gain information; I've interviewed professionals about the topic; I've given presentations about reputation management and personal branding; and I've had several articles about the concept published. And although I'm technically a marketer for a design firm, this topic relates directly to what I do for a living – even though few A/E/C marketers frame it the same way I do. So I'm differentiating myself and positioning myself as someone knowledgeable about the topic.

Don't be myopic and create false limitations regarding the topics you are qualified to write about. There's a lifetime's worth of potential content all around you right now.

The Tools:

- Company blog
- Personal blog
- Company newsletter
- Professional society newsletter
- Client organization newsletter
- A/E/C-related publication
- Industry-specific publication
- Local newspaper
- Regional business journal
- Books
- White papers

Tools Part 2: Building Your Reputation

Case Study: Holly Williams Leppo, AIA, LEED AP BD+C, NCARB, NCIDQ

Holly Williams Leppo is a partner and vice president of SMB&R in Camp Hill, Pennsylvania, where she oversees the firm's architectural department and continues to serve as a practicing architect and interior designer. She is licensed as an architect in several states, a LEED Accredited Professional with a Building Design + Construction specialization, and holds professional credentials from the National Council of Architectural Registration Boards and the National Council for Interior Design Qualification.

Holly has a long list of publishing credentials, including authorship of numerous technical review guides to prepare candidates for both the Architectural Registration Exam as well as the LEED credentialing exams. Her titles include *Construction Documents & Services*, *Building Design & Construction Systems*, *LEED Prep GA*, *LEED Prep ID&C*, *LEED Prep O&M*, and *LEED Prep BD&C*. With this background, Holly has been recognized as one of twenty-five Women of Influence by the *Central Penn Business Journal*, which also recognized her with a Forty Under 40 Award; she's also recipient of The Pennsylvania State University Alumni Association Alumni Achievement Award, Washington University Young Alumni Award of Distinction, and *Building Design + Construction* Forty Under 40 Award.

Holly began working with Professional Publications, Inc. – which has published all of her titles – shortly after taking the Architectural Registration Exam, initially serving as a technical reviewer. This opened the door for her a few years later, when the publisher contacted her about writing a study guide. How does Holly find time to write? She says, "My writing experience has been quick bursts of working furiously every evening and weekend, and then slower times when I am responding to errata, getting things ready for new editions ... so it is only an hour or two a month. It has so far worked very well with my personal and work schedule to be able to be involved in this way."

Writing has certainly made a difference in Holly's career. "My writing was first recognized by *Building Design + Construction* magazine's Forty Under 40 honor, and I think being featured in that publication led to other awards." The name recognition she gained in turn led to opportunities to become involved with her local chapter of the American Institute of Architects, selections committee for the Steele Architectural Scholarship, and Penn State College of Arts & Architecture Alumni Council. All this forms the backdrop for Holly's day job as vice president, architect, interior designer, and marketer for her firm, so she has been able to greatly expand her network and use her personal credentials to help differentiate SMB&R from their competitors.

Tools Part 2: Building Your Reputation

Case Study: Craig S. Galati, AIA, FSMPS, CPSM

Principal of LGA in Las Vegas, Craig is an architect with three decades of experience and a background in sustainability, architecture, and sociology. He has served as president of the AIA Nevada and AIA Las Vegas and is an active member of the Society for Marketing Professional Services, serving as SMPS Las Vegas President in 2009. Craig is a prolific writer and the author of three books, including *Business from the Heart; Lessons on Purpose, Passion, and Commitment*; *Admit It! 21 Things That You Already Knew But Apparently Have Forgotten About Client Service*; and *A Man in Transition; Reflections on Relationships, Leadership, and Life*.

While these three books have expanded Craig's reputation on a national level, he is also well-known to the Las Vegas business community as former author of the popular "The Heart of Business" blog. His writing has expanded his name recognition and been just one of the many personal branding tools that have helped Craig receive several prestigious awards, including the AIA Nevada Silver Medal, Las Vegas Chamber of Commerce Circle of Excellence Award, and *Nevada Business* magazine Most Respected CEO Award.

"The writing has helped me tremendously," says Craig. "I set out to use the blog to help me become a better writer, which it has. The interesting thing to me is how it has given me instant credibility with many new people that I meet," says Craig. "I've always been amazed at how many people read my blog and quote from my books. The writing has opened doors that I previously could not open." The writing credentials have also made him a sought-after speaker: "I am asked to speak more than I can fit into my schedule by many organizations on a variety of subjects." Furthermore, his books have led to numerous interviews in trade journals, which have in turn helped him land consulting and facilitation work.

Craig relays a story about a business trip. When he sat down on the plane he was surprised to find the passenger next to him reading *Business from the Heart*! "I had a very interesting conversation with him. He was a pool design consultant and had purchased the book from the Design Build Institute of America website."

Next Steps:

1. Research potential publications and obtain their editorial guidelines (usually available online).
2. Read past issues of the publications to determine whether or not they accept articles from outside sources (non-staff), the types of articles they prefer, and topics that have been recently published.
3. Write a query letter to the editor and pitch an idea or topic.
4. Submit a letter to the editor of your local newspaper or business journal, on a timely topic that is relevant to your industry.
5. Contact the organizations to which you belong (community, professional, client) and offer to write an article for their next newsletter or magazine.
6. Author an article for your company newsletter or blog.
7. Make a list of topics for a future book, and begin collecting notes, research, and stories related to that topic.

The Power of the Podium

I'm always amazed when I see highly accomplished professionals turn pale in terror at the thought of speaking in front of an audience. These professionals, of course, frequently have "the stage," and yet they don't even realize it. If you are in a meeting – even if only with one other person – then you are speaking in front of an audience. Design and construction professionals are *always* in meetings – scheduling meetings, team meetings, client meetings, quality review meetings, safety meetings. Have you ever thought to yourself, "Gee, I don't attend nearly enough meetings?" Of course not. We're all *meetinged* to death. Yet these same meetings we hate give us a platform for public speaking.

These meetings also provide a recurring means for building and maintaining our reputations. How do you react when others are listening? People remember confidence – they also remember when people are nervous, unprepared, argumentative, or unprofessional. It doesn't matter if you are serving on a committee at your firm or sitting across the table from your clients in a project meeting. You must always be on-game when in front of other people.

Standing up in front of an audience is not a natural behavior – everyone is staring at you. Fear of public speaking is so prevalent that it even has a name: glossophobia. You've probably heard public speaking referred to as our number one fear, ahead of death, snakes, and spiders. I don't buy it – I can think of a whole lot of fears that top public speaking. Don't get me wrong, I still get nervous in front of an audience, and most performers and speakers will tell you that they never feel totally comfortable no matter how many times they perform or speak.

But novice speakers can't help but feel that everyone is waiting for them to fail. Yet have you ever been in a presentation that went south because the speaker couldn't handle the pressure? They got too nervous, lost their place, began stuttering and sweating – almost waiting for a lifeline. As difficult as it is for the speaker, it is also rather awkward to be in the audience. It is tough watching the presentation derail – you almost feel voyeuristic to another person's misery, yet you can't turn away.

No one wants to see you fail. No one takes pleasure in watching it, so understand that everyone wants you to do well and succeed.

There are a number of low-impact ways to begin your public speaking journey. Speak at a company meeting, if only for two or three minutes. If you belong to a professional association or service group, offer to thank the sponsors or introduce the speaker. You'll still be speaking in front of an audience, but only for a few minutes.

Leading a training program at your company – frequently called a brown bag (if employees bring their own food) or lunch-n-learn (if food is served) because these trainings often occur over the lunch hour – is another way to get accustomed to speaking in front of an audience.

There are three things that you need to know about these programs. First, these are usually the easiest presentations to schedule. In fact, as you advance within a company, you may reach a level where it is expected that you give regular trainings, either within your department or company-wide.

Second, these trainings are a great ticket into the world of public speaking. You are given the opportunity to practice speaking in front of a group. You'll probably be standing in front of a seated audience. You may very well have graphic aids in the form of a PowerPoint, presentation boards, or model. You may be more comfortable in front of your co-workers because you feel that it doesn't matter as much if you don't do well.

Third, it really does matter how you perform. As it turns out, your co-workers may very well be the most difficult audience you face. They work with you on a daily basis and, face it, the workplace can be pretty competitive. Co-workers compare themselves to you. When you do well, it ups the pressure for them to perform.

Tools Part 2: Building Your Reputation

When you do poorly, they feel better about themselves and their position in the company. They are more likely to dissect your presentation, focusing on any perceived negatives. They are also the most likely to look disinterested. When you have the opportunity to speak at other forums, you'll find the people are typically more interested because they may be paying to attend and they may very well be there to meet you and hear your thoughts about the presentation topic. But with the internal company presentations, a lot of people are there because they are required to be or feel obligated to attend.

Doesn't that make you want to schedule a presentation in front of your co-workers next week?

You should. Musicians rehearse constantly. (Do you remember this old joke – "How do you get to Carnegie Hall? Practice, practice, practice.") Actors rehearse their scenes over and over again before they step on stage or in front of the camera. Talk show hosts usually do a run-through of their show before the audience arrives. Speakers regularly find ways to get in front of an audience. When you don't do it enough, you lose your mojo.

So make it a point to schedule yourself to get in front of your co-workers. Speak about a project case study. Give training on how to effectively use a software program. Share your experience in design or project management or construction administration or field work. And don't do it once and be done. Make it a regular part of your job, because it strengthens your speaking skills while enhancing your reputation with your co-workers (and supervisors).

Another great way to practice speaking in front of an audience is the "Rubber Chicken Circuit." The official definition of this phrase is a series of social gatherings with a traveling celebrity or politician giving a speech at each. "Rubber chicken" refers to the fact that a lot of people are dining, chicken is the most common meal, and because of the mass production, the chicken is pre-cooked and ends up rubbery. (I can't say for sure – I'm allergic to poultry. Talk about a conversation starter!) Many years ago I was invited to give a presentation about local architecture to one of the many Rotary Clubs in my community. At the time, I was serving on the board of a non-profit organization whose executive director was a regular speaker at Rotary clubs. She said, "Welcome to the Rubber Chicken Circuit." What is the circuit in your community? Rotary, Sertoma, Kiwanis, or Lions clubs, chambers of commerce, seniors groups – any organization that meets regularly, serves meals, and features a speaker at each meeting.

Does your particular area of expertise lend itself to a Rubber Chicken Circuit topic? Probably not. The way to become an expert is to focus on a niche, and these groups comprise people from all industries (and typically many retirees), so your core knowledge is not broad enough. So what should you speak about?

Is your firm involved with a project that is important to the community? Maybe you could co-present with your client about the project vision and benefits. If your company has reached a special milestone, maybe there is an opportunity to review corporate history and major project commissions. Perhaps there is a topic related to one of your hobbies – as long as it is something unique or something for which you have special credentials. For these groups, your presentation has to appeal to a broad audience.

As mentioned previously, I have an interest in historic architecture. The first several presentations I ever gave were actually marketing-related, given to local chapters of a professional marketing society. But as my self-study in local historic architecture grew, I began feeling comfortable about sharing my information with others. I spoke to several local Rotary Clubs, and then received an invite to speak at a nearby Rotary in another community. So I modified my presentation to feature several buildings in that particular community so it better related to the audience. Later I was invited back to the same organizations – and several more – to give a presentation about the community as pictured in old postcards.

The content was actually similar, but the first presentation was about architecture and featured current photos, while the second presentation was about history as viewed through the 50- and 100-year-old postcards. But a lot of the actual buildings pictured were the same for both presentations. I made a third round of presentations to the same groups, and others, presenting about the benefits of green preservation. And while the topic was significantly different than the first two, it still related to old buildings.

When you find a topic that works, modify and repackage! I've given more than 100 presentations to local organizations over the past few years. I've spoken to eight different Rotary Clubs, presenting four times at one club, other local service clubs, a postcard club, local builders association, community events, seniors groups, local colleges, retirement homes, and more. At these presentations, not once have I spoken on a topic directly related to my "day job" – marketing professional services. Still, these presentations allow me to practice and build my skills, try new things with presentation techniques, expand my local business network, and build/maintain my reputation.

Local chapters of professional associations and client organizations offer excellent venues for enhancing your reputation while building important credibility. While the Rubber Chicken Circuit presentations allow you to practice and gain name recognition locally, the professional associations provide a forum for showcasing your unique expertise. A topic only related to your core discipline might appeal to a specific organization, while one that ties your discipline to the other disciplines in a design and construction project might appeal to several organizations.

As a general rule, don't use industry jargon or get overly technical, unless you know that your audience will be able to understand you. Technical people tend to speak in their language, not in the language of their audience. So always remember to speak in terms that your audience will understand – this holds true whether you are speaking to co-workers, clients, or the audience of an organization or association.

As you develop a presentation, always develop it for the specific audience to which you are speaking. But then determine what else you can do with the presentation. If you give a highly-technical presentation to a focused audience, you are probably limited in where else you can give it. That is, unless you broaden your geography. If you gave the presentation to a local chapter of a national organization, are there other nearby local chapters – fifty or one hundred miles away?

For topics with a slightly broader appeal, but still A/E/C industry-related, there may be other organizations with local chapters. For instance, a presentation to a local chapter of the National Society for Professional Engineers may also be of interest to the local chapters of the American Institute of Architects, U.S. Green Building Council, and Associated Builders and Contractors. However, the presentation may require edits to tailor the information to each specific audience. A presentation about new applications for geothermal technology presented to an engineering organization may focus on the how's of doing it. A revised version of the presentation to the AIA, USBGC, and ABC may focus on the sustainable benefits, LEED points earned, and integration with other systems. Same content, different packaging.

If you're lucky, the presentation may have even broader appeal to a client organization, and you can speak to the local chapters of the International Facilities Management Association or APPA, an organization of higher education facilities officers.

Most organizations ask attendees to complete evaluations on the speakers. These forms typically ask some general information – appropriateness of cost, rating of venue, day and time, etc. Attendees are also asked to rate the speaker in terms of presentation abilities, knowledge of topic, and whether or not the presentation will be useful to their jobs. Once you speak and get the scores, it is totally appropriate to be nervous. After all, when you speak publicly, you put yourself out there for people to critique. While we naturally want positive reinforcement that we did a good job and provided value to the audience, negative comments can be beneficial as well. But remember, what you think is "negative" is rarely actually an attack on you, but constructive feedback that will help you better your presentation. Pay attention to those comments – don't change your presentation based upon one squeaky wheel (a single negative comment), but if there are a number of constructive comments about a specific issue, edit your presentation accordingly.

I speak a lot on the Society for Marketing Professional Services circuit, and have befriended many others who also regularly present to SMPS audiences. We've found that some of our marketing colleagues can be a bit more brutal with anonymous comments when compared with technical audiences. So my running joke is: How many SMPS members does it take to present? Fifty – one to present and 49 to say, "I could have done it better."

As for the positive comments, keep a database of quotes from attendees on your master resume (covered in the Additional Tools section) because you may need these for future applications to present at meetings or conferences.

Here's a tip: some of the most common responses from audiences are "more time for questions and answers" or "more interaction with audience." In other words, your audience doesn't just want to be spoken to – they want to feel like they are part of the presentation. I have one marketing presentation that includes a few musical snippets (great for after-lunch conference presentations to keep people awake!), and I often get positive feedback through comments like: "the music was a nice touch." It didn't make or break my presentation, but it was something *different*, so it stood out in people's minds.

As you begin to give presentations, hopefully you'll find a topic that is striking a chord with the audience. If you give the presentation several times, and receive continual positive feedback, this presentation is ideal to take to a larger audience. What associations have you given it to? Would this presentation appeal to a regional or national conference audience? What about other related associations?

You need to think about these presentations well in advance. Determine your target organizations, and visit their websites (or their conference websites, which are sometimes separate). Look for the "Call for Presentations," which will provide details about the information required as well as the deadlines. In some cases, the call will be released a year or more prior to the conference. Even if you don't plan to submit to speak at a conference right now, it is still worthwhile downloading the application form just to learn what information they are requesting. Some organizations require that shortlisted speakers submit videos of them presenting.

Typical questions are:

- Name of presentation
- Name of presenter
- Short overview of topic
- How the topic relates to the conference theme
- Presentation format (speech, workshop)
- List of previous presentations, including organizations presented to and scores
- Biography of presenter(s)

Why would you want to speak in front of your colleagues? Why would you want to educate the competition? For starters, it's just good form. We're all in this together, and competitors today may be teammates tomorrow. Presentations establish you as a thought leader in general and a leader in your specific industry. Future employers may be in the audience. Your supervisors may be impressed with your initiative, opening the door to new opportunities within your firm. Gaining a reputation as a talented speaker in your industry will help you and your company recruit new employees. Clients may be impressed with your speaking credentials, differentiating you, your company, and your team from the competition.

Ultimately, presentations build your brand, enhance your name recognition, and help you build your network. So there are myriad reasons to get out there and speak, but these presentations may actually open the door to something else.

In some ways, presentations to client organizations are the definitive opportunity for many design and construction professionals, because it puts them in front of potential clients. Ultimately, we all provide a service to clients and owners, so the opportunity to get in front of them and share knowledge is an excellent business development shortcut. When you speak to a client organization, you are able to showcase your expertise at something that is important to them – something that they need. The end-result may be that a prospective client or two seeks *you* out, something far more effective than cold calling, direct mail, advertising or any of the other high cost, low success sales and marketing approaches. Even if you and your firm are not awarded a contract that can directly be tied to a presentation, you are still out there, building name recognition, enhancing your brand, and adding a high-level credential to your portfolio. And keep in mind that on any given day, in any given year, most clients/owners don't need the services you offer. So you need to constantly position and reposition yourself, and stay in front of them, so that when the day comes that they need your services, you will be at the top of their minds.

After you speak to a client organization, ask for the attendance list. Follow up with attendees. Send them an article you wrote about the same topic as your presentation. Drop them a "thank-you for attending" note with your business card. Connect with them on social networks. Make sure they are in your CRM system. Remember, you've shared your expertise on a stage in front of them – you've differentiated yourself, and thus your company, from the countless competitors knocking on the clients' doors. Don't waste the opportunity!

When you present to a professional association or client organization, you may be asked to provide a PDF of your PowerPoint and any handouts. Don't worry about giving away your presentation – you are the presentation, not the handouts. But sending the slide deck to attendees afterward, with a short note, is a great excuse to follow-up. Do make sure your contact information appears in the document.

Throughout this chapter I've mentioned PowerPoint a few times because it is such an omnipresent tool for presenters. You may use Apple's Keynote, or the online alternative, Prezi, but in every case it is important that if you use the software, you use it to enhance your presentation, not distract from it. We've all sat through the 100-slide presentations with a dozen bullets per slide and few, if any, graphics. This snoozefest has played out millions of times across Corporate America and throughout the world. Technical professionals fill slides with their talking points. It helps them to feel more comfortable speaking. To tell the truth, I'd rather have horrible slides and a comfortable presenter than brilliantly-designed slides and a basket-case standing in front of audience. So there are tradeoffs.

First and foremost, do what makes you feel comfortable, at least for the first few times. No presenter wants to bore the audience to tears, of course, but if you view a presentation as your Carnegie Hall – and you practice, practice, practice to get there – you'll find that you really don't need those lengthy bullet points on the slides.

Don't get me wrong, bullet points are fully acceptable, but a few words are far superior to sentences. But why say it when you can show it? Graphics trump bullet lists, and a combination of powerful graphic and limited text may make the perfect slide. Studies have found that people only retain ten percent of what they hear, but 65% of what they hear and see.

There are some suggested rules out there that recommend that you limit your slides and talk for two or three or even five minutes per slide. We live in a short-attention span society raised on television and, more recently, YouTube. We're used to a constant barrage of images, so a static slide that stays on the screen for 300 seconds may seem like an eternity. Sometimes minimalism works. Other times a long parade of highly-visual slides can make a presentation interesting and dynamic.

It is easy to go overboard with animations and special effects. You've probably sat through a presentation or two that had so much movement and animation that you felt nauseous. However, a few select animations and slide transitions used consistently can add movement to the slides without making your audience feel like they just got off a rollercoaster.

For slide design, there are some excellent resources. Check out the *Presentation Zen* and *Slide:ology* books for great examples.

One technique that I've found effective is scripting my presentation. I build a rough outline of where I want to go with it, and then create really rough text-only slides that become my digital storyboard. I use PowerPoint, and rely on the Notes field for my script. I'll go through the presentation mentally, even reading my script aloud, making changes along the way. Then I'll turn my preliminary slides into visuals, using graphics and photos with as little text as possible to make the point. Next I'll rehearse again without the script, having it close at hand in case I need to reference it. By the time the presentation rolls around, I won't use any notes. For most people, presenting is much more natural that way. You're not constantly looking down at notes, you're not reading your slides and staring at the screen, and above all else, you're making regular eye contact with everyone in the audience. It is okay to reference your notes occasionally, so don't feel that you must memorize everything.

The benefit of including the script in the Notes field is that every time you give the presentation (because after you give it once, you'll want to take it on the road), you'll be able to reference the script to jog your memory. Often I only put bullet points in the Notes, but sometimes I actually write out the presentation. What I actually say changes each time I give the presentation, but at least I have a consistent base from which to practice. And when I repurpose the presentation, I use the same base file with all the Notes instead of beginning from scratch.

So what's holding you back … the audience is waiting!

The Tools:

- Company brown bag or lunch-n-learn
- Local service club (e.g., Rotary)
- Professional society – local
- Professional society – regional/national
- Client organization – local
- Client organization – regional/national
- College, university, or even high school

Tools Part 2: Building Your Reputation

Case Study: Scott W. Braley, FAIA, FRSA

Scott Braley has a long list of professional credentials, including Fellowship in both the American Institute of Architects and The Royal Society for the Encouragement of Arts, Manufactures and Commerce (UK). In the case of the latter, that puts him in a unique category alongside such well-known people as Benjamin Franklin and Charles Dickens. An architect by profession, Scott learned early that he had a penchant for managing projects and made that a focus of his career, eventually becoming Managing Principal in Heery International. There he worked closely with George Heery during the pioneering and developmental stages of the "bridging method" of project delivery. One of his most famous projects was Atlanta's Georgia Dome, which when built was the largest rigid-cable dome structure in the world. With this background, Scott received a Medal of Excellence from *ENR Magazine*.

Today he is a consultant, helping design and construction firms with strategy, leadership, marketing, project delivery, and a host of other services. But during his time with Heery, Scott developed a passion for public speaking, and soon began teaching project managers at several annual Project Management Bootcamp sessions. He was later able to leverage his speaking skills and vast network of contacts and create a business by reaching out to industry organizations and becoming a sought-after speaker. In recent years he has given presentations to national conferences of more than twenty industry organizations. These include the Society for Marketing Professional Services (SMPS), American Consulting Engineers Council (ACEC), American Institute of Architects (AIA), Society of American Military Engineers (SAME), American Society of Interior Designers (ASID), International Facilities Management Association (IFMA), Associated General Contractors of America (AGC), National Society of Professional Engineers (NSPE), and others.

Scott is very proud of his project accomplishments, and believes that, "By speaking and talking about my current work and experiences, two things happened. One, the attention to the project work was sparked. Two, the association with 'the work and the person' was made more real and more evident. It's one thing to read about a project, it's quite another to speak with someone who can answer questions. The synergy of worthwhile accomplishment and the person speaking has the side effect of heightening the level of attention to the work as well as the reputation of the person involved."

Throughout his career, Scott has been able to use his public speaking abilities not just to generate new work opportunities, but also to benefit his clients. On one occasion, he was asked to present to a powerful corporate board of directors on behalf of his client. On another, Scott found himself on the front pages of newspapers after he was asked to unveil the design for Olympic Stadium in Atlanta. Although he has spoken to audience of all sizes throughout much of the United States, he still focuses on making every presentation a unique experience: "Even with a lot of public speaking experience, I still do not take it for granted – I take each engagement seriously, and consequently have pre-session jitters every time!"

Next Steps:

1. Research speaking opportunities at the local level and contact Rotary Clubs, Sertoma Clubs, and other organizations that regularly need speakers.
2. Contact the local chapters of professional associations and client organizations and inquire about the process for speaking to their groups.
3. Research the websites for national professional and client organizations to learn about their national confer-

ences — most usually post a "Call for Presentations" months before the next scheduled conference or event.

4. Research presentation topics — what has already been given? What would be a good potential topic for a targeted audience?

5. Develop a "onesheet" that provides a brief biography with your credentials, list of potential presentation topics, and list of previous presentations (topics or organizations).

6. Offer to lead a company brown bag session on a topic of value to your co-workers.

7. Purchase and read a book like *Presentation Zen* by Garr Reynolds or *Slide:ology* by Nancy Duarte to learn the difference between a good PowerPoint and a poor PowerPoint.

8. Enroll in a Toastmasters or Dale Carnegie course to learn to become a better presenter.

Making News Instead of Reading It

This tool is about thought leadership and media relations. When you become a thought leader, the media opportunities increase. Being quoted in a newspaper or magazine article builds credibility by establishing you as an expert on a particular topic.

There are several paths you can take to build your reputation through the media.

The first thing to understand is that all media – particularly print and online, which are more prevalent than radio and television in our industry – need content. Continually. If you can help them find content, they will be appreciative.

If a reporter calls your office asking for information, by all means help them. If they want a quote about a topic that you're not really qualified to talk about, be honest. Tell them and then recommend someone they can talk with or another source for information. And if you are, in fact, qualified to discuss the topic at hand, give them something they can use.

Offer to follow up with an email (you're less likely to be misquoted) with additional information. If the reporter is probing about a project you are working on, that's okay. They are just doing their job. But if you don't feel comfortable talking about the project without your client's knowledge, politely decline to provide information, but help the reporter get in touch with the client. And if you have a non-disclosure agreement, you have the perfect out: "I'd love to help you, but I'm under a confidentiality agreement."

But why, exactly, would the media contact you in the first place?

Often, reporters reach out to design and construction professionals when they get wind of a project. Institution A is expanding, Company B is relocating, Municipality C is planning a new road. A reporter has been given the assignment to write an article, so they begin snooping around to find out project information. Often, this leads them to the selected designer or constructor, and they work

Tools Part 2: Building Your Reputation

their way through the firm until they find the proper person to interview. If this is you, there will be an immediate decision to make: is it okay to discuss the project? If your company signed a non-disclosure agreement (NDA), you can't say anything. But even if that agreement isn't in place, you still have to make a gut call. This isn't a time to "act now, ask for forgiveness later" – you don't want to risk damaging your relationship with the client. So it is often acceptable to say that you need the client's permission before you talk to the reporter. However, as soon as you do this, you need to contact your client to discuss the interview. Establish parameters for what is acceptable to discuss – or get the contact information of the individual within your client's organization who will gladly talk with the reporter.

It is important to be helpful to the reporter but not compromise your client relationship in the process.

However, there are other times when a reporter might contact you. Sometimes they are simply trying to find out the correct person to interview, so they work their database. They may very well contact you knowing that you won't be their ultimate source of information, but they believe that you can help direct them to that source. Again, be helpful. Do not view the reporter as one who is interrupting your day – view them as someone that can become an important component in your reputation-building process. If you help them today, they may be able to help you in the future. There are times when I've been at home at night, after my son has gone to bed, and a reporter has called. Other times I've been on vacation when my cell phone rang and a reporter was on the other end. There have been times when I've spent thirty or more minutes on the telephone helping a reporter, never getting quoted but yet seeing my input in the article they wrote. Other times I'll be quoted, but it will be very short and sweet. On some occasions, I've specifically asked not to be quoted, but provided non-confidential information to a reporter – or given them alternative contacts to go to for a quote. I'm building a relationship in the process.

This is critical, because when building a reputation, there will be times when you will need help from the media. And "media" is a somewhat nebulous term that encompasses just about every news source, so boil it down to the individual reporters and editors. Give them a reason to contact you, interview you, or quote you.

In previous chapters I've touched upon innovation and research. Try something different or unique. Delve into a topic and conduct primary research through surveys and interviews. This is perhaps the quickest way to establish yourself as a thought leader. When you have something "different" to say, you become newsworthy. You have content for articles and blogs and white papers. You have a topic of interest to professional organizations or client associations. And you have reason for media to contact you. Writing an article builds your credibility, but so does being quoted in a newspaper or industry periodical. When you read a quote in a newspaper or magazine, you automatically assume that person is an expert on the topic they are discussing.

I've met a lot of innovative thinkers who don't think that they are doing anything unique or special. They are just doing what they were trained to do. So they walk around with blinders on, limiting themselves. But then they read an article or attend a conference and see another professional talking about something "new" or "innovative" – even though they may have done something similar a year or two earlier. It is only when that happens that they realize, "Hey, I should have been more vocal about this when I was working on it." In general, architects are better promoters than engineers or constructors. It's said that in product branding you don't have to be best, you just have to be first. But in personal branding, a lot of times the professionals that are there first keep it a secret. So they lose out on building their reputations as thought leaders.

Tools Part 2: Building Your Reputation

Smokey the Bear famously stated, "Only you can prevent forest fires." To paraphrase the talking black bear: "Only you can establish yourself as a thought leader." Sure, marketing and PR departments, colleagues, media, professional associations, writing, speaking – these can all help in the process. But you must be the first one to say, "Hey, this is unique! Check it out!" If your company has a marketing department, don't just expect them to know. Tell them!

Think about when LEED came onto the scene and no one knew much about it. But then you read in your local newspaper that a competitor designed a LEED Certified building – the first in the area. And then you read about a local architect – or engineer or construction manager – earning LEED Accredited Professional status. They earned publicity for it because they were first. Today, thousands of projects have earned LEED certification and more than 100,000 professionals have earned the LEED AP designation. Its newsworthiness has declined over the past decade.

Along came the Cascadia Region Council's Living Building Challenge, providing a whole new level of sustainable buildings. Some firm, or some person, had to be first to design a building to the rigid new criteria. First in the country. First in the region. First in the state. First in the city.

Not to mention first house, first school, first office, etc.

This is newsworthy – earning media attention for those individuals and firms that were early adopters. But as the Living Building Challenge grows in popularity, its newsworthiness will decline.

Sustainability continues to evolve, however. The American High Performance Buildings Coalition was formed to lobby against the U.S. Green Building Council's LEED program. Some states dropped LEED certified project requirements. The U.S. General Services Administration broadened their sustainability program to include the rising Green Globes program.

Suddenly there was another new opportunity to be first in sustainable design and construction. First Green Globes certified project in the country, region, state, or city. Or first office, school, house, etc. Or first certified Green Globes Professional (GGP) or Green Globes Assessor (GGA) – in your community or market space.

The point here is that the industry is in a continual state of evolution, so if you miss one thought leadership bus, another is certainly coming behind it. You must be astute of the trends and opportunities in your profession and in the markets you serve.

When you are an early adopter, or have compiled unique research, you must leverage that to create news, and develop relationships with media by establishing yourself as a subject matter expert on a given topic.

The Tools:

- Press releases
- Interviews with media
- Surveys
- Research reports
- Thought leadership & innovation

Case Study: J. Timothy Griffin, PE, CEM, LEED AP, CBCP

Tim Griffin knows the Millennial generation. As a director and regional manager of RMF Engineering's Raleigh, North Carolina and Atlanta, Georgia offices, he's worked with quite a few members of the younger generation of the workforce. These personal experiences developed in him an interest about "What makes Millennials tick?" Through the discovery process, Tim soon found that he had a book in him, authoring *Winning with Millennials: How to Attract, Retain & Empower Today's Generation of Design Professionals*, which was published by Design Leadership Press in 2009. His research and interviews with design and construction professionals also opened the door for him to consult with A/E/C organizations across North America on the topic of Millennials and created opportunities to speak on the topic at industry conferences. But it also firmly established Tim as a thought leader on the subject – the go-to expert when media needs a quote from an established authority. Tim has been quoted in *Metal Architecture*, *PSMJ Best Practices*, *Sources + Design*, *Engineering Inc.*, and publications of the American Consulting Engineers Council, to name a few.

RMF Engineering is a mechanical, electrical, and plumbing engineering firm, and Tim is a licensed engineer, certified energy manager, LEED accredited professional, and certified building commissioning professional. Not exactly the person you'd naturally expect to be the go-to expert for researching generational behavior in the workplace! Yet, this is a topic that Tim is passionate about, and his sincerity comes through in his writing and interviews. He exemplifies thought leadership, and was really the first A/E/C professional to embrace and research this subject in depth, creating a very positive personal brand in the process. As you can imagine, he also has a much easier time recruiting Millennials to his firm when compared with other MEP and A/E firms – many of which are still adverse to the concepts of social media and flexible schedules, two major attractors of the younger generation. As Tim states, "The book has given me a way to connect with Millennials, help them, and build strong relationships that have benefited our company. Also, in multiple cases I have had mid-level to senior engineers read the book and want to come work for me because it spoke to them on a core level."

The benefits of researching and writing the book have been many. In addition to being regularly invited to speak on the subject at industry conferences, Tim has found that his thought leadership "Opened doors within my own organization and within other organizations to influence positive change in ways that were not possible before." Additionally, Tim has built a network of people from around the world because of his book.

"My advice from this experience, and others, is always jump on any opportunity you get that is outside of your traditional work role. The scarier the better. If you are a design architect or engineer, when opportunities come along to market, travel, speak publicly, write an article, serve on a trade organization's committee, etc., jump on it. If the opportunity scares you, all the better. It is those opportunities that stretch you, prepare you for greater opportunities of influence, and open doors. They also give you a wider and more accurate view of the world."

Next Steps:

1. Research media opportunities – where have you seen articles in which you could have provided valuable information and insight?
2. Reach out to reporters and offer to become an expert resource on a topic they regularly write about.
3. Research potential topics – new trends, changes in products, best practices – topics that are not well-

represented in publications but would be of interest to them.

4. Conduct surveys or undertake primary research on one of these topics.

5. Publish your findings in a white paper, blog, book, or ebook.

6. Create fact sheets highlighting your findings.

7. Prepare and send press releases about your findings to relevant media.

8. Provide talking points (short tidbits with meaningful information) to media, co-workers, colleagues, etc.

9. Connect media with your sources, even if it means that you won't be quoted (the favor will be returned at a later date, possibly multiple times over).

10. Provide graphics, backgrounders, or other information to media, when requested and in a timely fashion (reporters usually work on extremely tight deadlines).

Virtual Reality: Knowledge Sharing & Networking from Your Office Chair

Anyone who has worked in the design and construction business for more than twenty years can remember the "pre-Internet" era. Communication was vastly different because we relied on conversations – on the telephone, in person. Project communications were via memos and carbon copied forms. Research was conducted in libraries. Blue prints were actually blue.

Then e-mail came along, but it took a while to filter through the industry. It was crude by today's standards, of course, but it fundamentally changed the way we did business. And then we discovered that there was a world beyond America Online – this fascinating new thing called the Internet. Our marketing approaches changed and adapted to technological advancements. Websites went from non-existent to awful to tolerable yet static to interesting and dynamic.

Seemingly out of nowhere, social networking and media upended things. Suddenly the web was a *conversation*, not just a *lecture*. This technology has created a whole new world centered on free, easy-to-use technology that connects us with dozens, hundreds, or even thousands of people. Instantly.

Talk about a great tool for building and maintaining your reputation!

Your company website can be a brand-building tool, but only if you have a presence on it. If you appear in the "Key Staff" section, you probably have a brief bio there for the world to see. Make sure it accurately reflects who you are and what you do – and includes a recent photograph of you. A lot of corporate website bios are lacking in useful, interesting content, meaning that your company has missed a great opportunity to market the firm through elevating employee personal brands.

Tools Part 2: Building Your Reputation

If you are not on the company website, should you be?

Or perhaps there is another way. Does your company have a blog? If so, are you blogging on it? Blogs (short for weblogs) are short articles that can establish your expertise and create your reputation as a thought leader. Blogs can expand your network because once your byline is out there, people will reach out to you – by email, phone, or social networking sites. Blogs can lead to invitations to speak or author articles for publication in print or online periodicals. In fact, some of the blogs I wrote originally for my company website ended up being re-published in industry periodicals or other blogs. Plus, you will begin appearing in Google searches. People research you before, or after, they meet with you. You are being Googled right now. Blogs also drive traffic to your website. In fact, they often serve as the "front door" because visitors find your blog through Internet searches. If they like what they see on your blog, they may look around, checking out other pages and learning more about your company.

If you blog, you build your personal brand while also marketing the company.

Many professionals I've spoken with have stated outright that they don't know how to get started, and that they don't really have any topics worth writing about. But that is extremely far from the truth. Here are a few ideas:

Blog about a recent project you were involved with, but be wary of confidential information. It is acceptable to be generic and use a phrase like, "a recent project for a regional hospital" instead of "a recent project for Acme Regional Medical Center."

Maybe you've come across an interesting new product – something you've specified or installed in the field. Blog about it. How did you use it? What are its unique features? Did it earn LEED points?

Blog about a client or vendor – what kind of interesting things are they doing? Make sure they are aware of your blog before it is posted – and ask for a quote and a photograph: help build their personal brands!

What kind of trends are you seeing – in the design and construction industry in general, or in a specific market segment in which you have expertise? If you can provide news-to-use to your clients, you'll add depth to your reputation as an expert in their field.

Sustainability is one of the most popular topics for design and construction professionals to blog about. In fact, some A/E/C firms have blogs dedicated to green buildings.

Lessons learned are a personal favorite of mine. Anyone can blog about a new product, but only you can blog about your lessons learned. Your unique personal experiences have built your knowledge base, and you may have come across some distinct information that is worth sharing. Remember, some of the worst project experiences make for the most interesting stories.

Repurpose your content liberally. Did you write an article for a company or organization newsletter? Use it, or a variation of it, in your blog. Did you lead a company lunch-n-learn or speak to a professional association or client organization? Take the content and write a blog – or a series of blogs – about it.

How many times have you written a detailed e-mail about something – a process, advice, recommendation, or explanation about something? This e-mail, though probably only meant for one or a few individuals, could be tailored to a blog post.

Blog about your thought-leading activities. Did you conduct a survey or series of interviews about a specific topic or trend? Blog about it.

I was invited to speak at a regional real estate symposium hosted by a business journal. A lot of time was spent developing the presentation, and I created detailed notes in the process. After the program, I turned those presentation notes into a series of blog posts – and later, into an ebook.

Tools Part 2: Building Your Reputation

Like any of the reputation-building tools, you will need to commit time. Daniel Kerr, PE, a prolific blogger and current president of Burns Mechanical, often writes his blog posts early on Saturday mornings. Find a time and environment that works best for you, and be consistent. And remember, you're not writing *War and Peace*. A blog post could be 300-500 words. Plus, if your company already has a blog, you may only need to contribute a few times a year. But understand that the more you blog, the more your name gets dispersed and the quicker you begin to build a name for yourself (a.k.a., reputation).

Confession: I still have trouble selling the value of blogging to some colleagues. They "get it" conceptually, at least, but still don't view it is a core function. So I've tried to help them and demonstrate value by writing a few ghost blogs. My company had worked on several major projects where manufacturing clients wanted LEED certified buildings. But in most cases, their process energy requirements to run the production equipment were so high that it was cost-prohibitive to implement alternative energy or purchase green energy. In these cases the clients didn't believe that they could justify the added expense to their boards of directors, and opted for buildings with sustainable features but no certification.

It was a message that I really thought needed to get out there, because at the time there was not a lot about LEED and manufacturing on the Internet. So I interviewed one of our project managers on a Friday afternoon. We spent about fifteen minutes together at the end of the work day, and he looked through the LEED scorecards and told me about all the challenges for each project. The following Monday morning, I took the notes, did some extra research, and drafted a blog for him. It was actually 1500 words (long for a blog), but was full of lessons learned. The project manager reviewed it, corrected a few things, added some new content, and we posted the blog under his name.

Several weeks later I passed him in the hall and he stopped me and said, "You're not going to believe this…" Well, a national organization was looking into LEED certification and manufacturing challenges, and was gathering data. They did a Google search, and his blog post came up. So they picked up the telephone and called him, picking his brain. One blog post and suddenly he was building a reputation as a thought leader in sustainable manufacturing facilities.

After we spoke I Googled "LEED, manufacturing," and sure enough, his blog post was the first listing – above the U.S. Green Building Council! We repurposed his blog post as a newsletter targeting manufacturers, and sent it out shortly thereafter. I can't promise such instant results for you (or me, to be honest!), but it is a great example of the power of blogging in building one's reputation.

But your bio is not on the company website and your company doesn't even have a blog. What should you do?

Increasingly, professionals in all industries are turning to personal websites and blogs. Most social media experts recommend that you at least reserve your domain name now. My personal website is www.scottbutcher.com. Even if you don't create a website immediately, at least own your name.

It wasn't that long ago that you needed to use specialized software programs to build an aesthetically-pleasing website. For the professional web designers that might have been Dreamweaver, and for the hacks (like me) it was Microsoft FrontPage. There were web hosts that had some basic templates, but they were unattractive and cumbersome.

And then along came blogging and blogging platforms, and they pretty much changed the game. People and companies realized that they didn't need to spend $10,000 or $50,000 to get a professional-looking website. They could use WordPress and build a "website" on a blogging platform. They could be the web designers themselves, using countless attractive templates. Within a day or two, they could create a website that effectively marketed their company or themselves. This doesn't change the important role that specialized web design firms play when you need a customized or unique web presence or advanced Search Engine Optimization (SEO) capabilities, but it did simplify web design to the extent where most people could create an attractive site with little effort or cost.

I actually learned about WordPress in an article encouraging writers to build simple and attractive websites through WordPress. And while there is a free version of the software, your content will be hosted elsewhere (the www.wordpress.com website), and thus you'll be directing traffic away from your website. However, there are countless web hosts that have WordPress built into their packages. This is preferable, because you will be the host, driving traffic to your website.

Here's how inexpensive things have become. I built my personal website for $135, paying $100 for a one-year hosting plan with Yahoo! Small Business and $35 for an attractive WordPress template. It took a weekend to build my personal website and then I came into the office on Monday and set about redoing the company website. When I purchased the template for my personal site, I did so with the thought that it would work for the company website. So we ditched our web host (they didn't offer WordPress plans), opened a hosting account with another company, downloaded the same template, and built a new website.

I'm not a web designer – nor is anyone on my marketing team. But WordPress is *easy*, which is why I recommend it. There are hundreds – thousands – of resources on the Internet to get you started and walk you through the process. My point here is that you own your reputation, and you can build it by creating a personal website and blog.

My personal website has bit of everything. It promotes my books. It promotes my photography. It promotes my presentations.

It promotes me as a professional services marketer. And it promotes my firm and drives traffic to the company website.

Some people view having a personal website as radical or even narcissistic, but it is really more akin to having a personal resume and a profile on social media sites. So if you aren't ready to make the jump to a personal blog or website, make sure you are on the social networking websites.

If there is one place you need to be, it is LinkedIn. This social networking site is for business professionals just like you. You may already have a profile, but are you doing anything with it?

I've met so many great contacts through LinkedIn – it is an awesome networking tool. One of my favorite social media stories relates to LinkedIn. I received a connection request from someone in Texas. She worked for a company that provided software for A/E/C marketers. Whenever someone in the industry reaches out to me, I accept their invitation to connect. It doesn't matter where they are, or what they do. Every connection is valuable – even if it doesn't seem so at first.

So I accepted her invitation, and then immediately looked over her LinkedIn profile to figure out who she was and why she might want to connect. Plus, with most people posting photos on their profile, it always helps to put a face with a name.

Two days later I traveled to Houston to speak at a conference. By the time I reached the hotel, I was famished, and the opening reception was still several hours away. So I meandered down to the hotel bar and ordered lunch. A few minutes later a woman walked in and sat a few stools over from me. I noticed that she was wearing a name tag with the SMPS logo on it, and since I was there to speak at a regional SMPS conference, I turned to introduce myself.

But I already knew her ... and she already knew me. It turned out that she was the one who had sent the LinkedIn invitation to connect a few days earlier. We recognized each other immediately, laughed about it, and had lunch together. Her company was one of the sponsors, and I've since networked with her at other SMPS events.

If you believe virtual networking to be a waste of time, change your thinking immediately. Your virtual network not only enhances your real-world network, but owners have told A/E/C audiences that they are using LinkedIn to learn about people who they are meeting with, or people being proposed for their project teams.

LinkedIn is a phenomenal tool for building a virtual network – but only if you use it to its fullest potential.

If you don't have an account, get one now. (It's free – you don't need a Premium Account to get a lot of value from LinkedIn.) Complete your profile. And by "complete," I actually mean *complete*. I am connected with many design and construction professionals that have only entered bare-bones information. When you do this, you limit the personal branding potential of LinkedIn and thus reduce its value as a networking tool.

The Summary section is important as it gives you a chance to provide a concise overview of who you are – your background, talents, capabilities, and experience. It is essentially your personal brand statement – the commercial for *brand you*.

Include your work experience – present and past. (Listing past employers gives former co-workers and even clients a means to find you.) Some people include professional association involvement under the Experience section; however, there is another section for that. List Honors and Awards that you've received. These can be personal awards, or awards for projects on which you were a team member. Complete the Volunteer Experience & Causes section to showcase your community involvement, and then complete the Organizations section to demonstrate your involvement with professional associations and client organizations. The Skills & Expertise section allows you to share what you know with the world. Include technical skills, management skills, industries served, etc. You'll find that soon your connections will begin endorsing you for your skills. If you've ever had anything published – even in a local chapter newsletter of your professional association – include it in the Publications section. Add a description and link if it is available online. Add professional licenses and certifications under the Certifications section. List degrees and even major continuing education endeavors under the Education tab.

The Additional Information tab allows you to list professional and personal interests, and more – be sure to complete it. Then add your personal information as well as personal details. Make sure you add your contact information including business address, email, and telephone number. Why do this? It not only gives people a way to contact you, but a lot of smartphones today, and even Microsoft Outlook, can integrate with LinkedIn and automatically download your Connections. This is an incredibly convenient feature.

If you have a Twitter account, connect it with your LinkedIn account.

There is another tab, Recommendations, which will be covered under the Referrals and Testimonials section of this book.

Upload your photo. People want to see you. As one social media consultant stated, "Your photograph is your personal logo." Make sure it is a professional photo. While it may be obvious to not use that old photo of you doing a keg stand, understand that you need a professional portrait. The setting can be informal, and you don't need to be dressed to the nines, but it should reinforce your brand, not detract from it. Don't take a photo of you and some friends, or co-workers, and crop your head out. Don't use a photo that is so dark that we can't even make out your face. Don't use an image of you standing in front of a tree with a branch "growing" out of your head. Think press release here – what type of photograph would you want sent with a press release about you? It is worth spending a few dollars and getting a professional portrait – or even running to the local Sears or mall photo studio to get a well-exposed image with a neutral background. And men, as tempting as it may be to use a photo of you with more hair (I'm with you on this), use a recent image.

Once your profile is complete, start making connections. Who do you know? Or want to know? Reach out to co-workers, vendors, and friends. Search for your clients and connect with them if they're on LinkedIn. Go through your Outlook address book and see if those contacts are on LinkedIn. Find the people you regularly interact with at community groups, professional associations, and client organizations. When someone accepts your invitation to connect, review their information in depth. Has anything changed (new position, new employer, etc.) since you last communicated with them? Then, check out their connections. This is one of the great tools of LinkedIn – you can use your connections for introductions to their connections, and vice-versa.

If I want to learn about someone, or meet someone, I'll first see if they are on LinkedIn. If so, what information can I glean from their Public Profile? Some people allow a lot of information to be shown to anyone, others limit most of their information and only allow their connections to see the details. I'll see if any of my connections are connected to them – that way I can communicate with my connections and ask about the person I want to meet with. Maybe I'll ask for an introduction, or perhaps I'll try to just gain additional intelligence.

The next step is to join Groups. If you belong to any community, professional, or client organizations, check to see if they have LinkedIn Groups, then join them. There may be a national Group for a given organization, as well as Group for your local chapter. Some organizations create LinkedIn Groups for forthcoming conferences as a way to share information, including who is attending. Seek out Groups that relate to your passions and interest and hobbies. Join your local chamber of commerce's Group, and then join Groups that relate to your clients' industries.

Why should you join Groups?

To broaden your network and meet new people. Being in a Group with someone else is also an excuse to invite them to be a connection. Furthermore, Groups have discussions, and by participating in these discussions – and sharing your knowledge – you will be further building your reputation as an expert. Once you begin participating in the discussions, asking and answering questions, you'll find that people want to connect with you and even have sidebar discussions.

If you can't find a Group related to a topic of interest, start one. It's easy to do, and can open new doors for finding connections. I started an industry-related human resources group on LinkedIn for a colleague who wanted to get in touch with other HR managers in the design and construction industry. It is not a big group, but it does offer a forum for asking questions and helping others with their issues.

These are just some of the tools within LinkedIn. Spend time familiarizing yourself with everything LinkedIn has to offer. Be sure to share regular updates about what you are working on. These updates provide insight into you, and can also be effective brand-building tools. For instance, if you write a blog post, you can share a link to it via a LinkedIn Update. Or share that you've been scheduled to speak somewhere. Or post a link to an article about a project you are working on.

On your LinkedIn homepage you'll be able to read recent updates posted by other members of your network. Be sure to read these regularly to know what your connections are doing, which ones have new positions or new employers, and more. The feed will also let you know when someone updates their profile, or changes their photo.

Yes, it does seem like stalking.

Tools Part 2: Building Your Reputation

No, it is not stalking, because they are providing that information with full knowledge that you, and their hundreds of other connections, will be seeing it.

Now, if the LinkedIn sections sound familiar, they should. Many of the reputation-building tools found in this book have direct parallels with the LinkedIn sections. Why? Because this stuff works. It works for design and construction professionals. It works for professional services marketers. It works for businesspeople and writers and recording artists and politicians and non-profit leaders.

Another social networking tool is Twitter. I was pretty skeptical about Twitter when it launched – after all, why would I want to read about what someone ate for breakfast? That's the perception of Twitter. The reality is far different. I've connected with a lot of thought leaders who provide information to me daily. (So much information that I cannot keep up with it.) I follow a lot of people in the A/E/C industry as well as my local community. My Twitter connections are constantly Tweeting insightful comments and links of interest, often to industry-related articles or blogs. I follow industry media and local media alike, and Twitter has become an excellent news source. I've Tweeted questions and received thoughtful answers. I've actually been invited to speak at a conference because of Twitter! Here are a few quick steps to get you going.

Create an account, and set up a Twitter handle that is consistent with your other social media sites (I'm scottdbutcher on LinkedIn, Twitter, Facebook, and YouTube). Complete your "headline," which is your 140-word bio. Upload a *current* photo and include a link to your website (company or personal). Or link to your LinkedIn profile.

Begin following colleagues, friends, competitors, vendors, clients, prospects, design and construction firms, A/E/C media, local media, and community contacts.

Listen. Read what others are posting. Follow their links. Once you are on Twitter, the first thing you need to do is learn. Learn what makes content interesting. Learn the unique lingo being used. Learn how to post something of value in 140 characters or less – the key to Twitter.

Do searches using the # symbol. In Twitter jargon, these are known as hashtags. If someone posts about building information modeling and follows it with #BIM, they are making that content appear in any related searches. The hashtag feature is actually very powerful as it allows you to find myriad content, and new people to follow, based upon topics of interest to you. If you want your post to reach members of an organization, for instance (beyond your followers), the # function provides a way to do it. For example, if I post something related to professional services marketing, I might end my post with #SMPS and #AEC. Both are common hashtags that allow my post to appear in SMPS and AEC searches.

And by search, I'm not just referring to using the search feature on Twitter. There are many third-party dashboards like Hootsuite and Tweedeck that allow you to combine several social media accounts into a single monitoring station. For instance, I monitor #AEC, #BIM, #AIA, #SMPS, and a number of other industry-related hashtags.

The hashtag for my local community is #iloveyorkcity, so I monitor that one, too. If I'm speaking to a local organization, I might Tweet something like, "I'll be speaking about local architecture at the downtown Rotary Club in #iloveyorkcity next Wednesday," and include a link to the announcement. Links can be very long – and in Twitter you are limited to 140 characters, so there are a number of free URL shortening services that you can use, like Bit.ly.

Once you begin feeling comfortable with Twitter, begin posting content. It's okay to begin slowly. It's acceptable to post something about you or your company, but post more often about others. Retweet interesting observations (A Retweet is when you share some-

Tools Part 2: Building Your Reputation

one else's Tweet with your followers). Tweet links to articles you've read or industry news or cool stuff you've come across online.

Pew Research published a list of what people Tweet about. Here are the top nine topics:

- o Personal updates
- o Work updates
- o Links to news
- o General observations
- o Retweet others
- o Direct message (when you contact someone directly via Twitter)
- o Share photos
- o Share videos
- o Tweet location

Part of being active with Twitter is following more people. Standard etiquette is that once someone follows you, you should follow them back. But this is not a hard and fast rule. You'll find many people that follow you specifically so you will follow them because they want to sell you something! Likewise, not everyone you follow will follow you back. However, when you follow media, they will often follow you back. So when you post news or a blog link or an interesting observation, you may in fact be giving them an idea or a reason to contact you about a story they happen to be working on.

Facebook is another social media platform that you can use to build your brand. It was originally a tool for college students to communicate, but spread far beyond the collegiate world and became a part of people's everyday lives. For many, it became a way to stay in contact with their family and friends (or former classmates that they haven't seen in several decades). Then the business world saw great value in Facebook, and companies that produced consumer-oriented products and services jumped on the bandwagon. Today, an increasing number of business-to-business organizations are building their Facebook presence.

Most professionals and A/E/C companies focus more on LinkedIn than Facebook, although that is changing. Some A/E/C companies maintain Facebook pages for their employees to communicate with one another and share company news and activities, particularly in the cases of companies with multiple offices. Firms in the design and construction industry also utilize Facebook for recruitment, particularly for college students and members of the Millennial generation.

If you follow the guidelines for LinkedIn and Twitter, you'll be able to handle Facebook; however, keep in mind that many people use Facebook for personal connections, so a client or colleague that may be willing to connect with you on LinkedIn may not want to connect with you on Facebook. Furthermore, people tend to let their guard down a bit when posting on Facebook; however, if you are connected with other professionals – be they clients or coworkers or industry contacts or community leaders – you need to be very wary about what you post. The web is filled with countless horror stories of employees losing jobs or companies losing clients because of comments made on social media sites, and people who maintain their professional façade on LinkedIn or Twitter sometimes don't do the same with Facebook. If you are on Facebook, be sure to check your privacy settings – your information may be open for anyone to see, so those comments or photos that you think are only being seen by your Facebook friends may in fact be open to the world.

Be aware that you can be tagged in other people's photos. So even if you aren't the one posting something on a social media site, someone may take a photo of you, post it on their account, and tag you – meaning that it will appear on your social media stream. The world is watching you, whether you like it or not!

Tools Part 2: Building Your Reputation

A family member, as she approached college graduation, changed her social media names because of fears that potential employers may be Googling her and learning a wee bit too much about her personal life. But the Internet remembers, and once something is out there, it is hard to get rid of it. Just check out the Way Back Machine Internet Archive, which visits websites and makes copies for future reference. So that horrible first attempt at a company or personal website may still be online somewhere! Check it out here: http://archive.org/web/web.php.

YouTube is yet another social media platform, but one that focuses exclusively on video. More and more professionals are using video as a means to build their reputations, and YouTube is the most popular medium for sharing their message. Plus, you can post a video on YouTube and then embed it in your website. You can also use tools like SlideShare and Google Presentation to embed videos on your LinkedIn Profile.

"Video" is a loose term on the web. It obviously refers to the true "motion picture" definition, but also includes animated slideshows created in PowerPoint, Producer, iMovie, or other video editors.

YouTube accounts are free and allow you to post a seemingly endless parade of videos. In general, videos are limited to 15 minutes in length, though you can request approval to post longer videos.

How can a video build your reputation?

To answer that, just think of all the opportunities there are for videos.

- o Animated slideshow of projects you designed (portfolio presentation)
- o Video of you giving a presentation
- o Video of you talking to the camera about a topic relevant to your expertise

- Video of your client talking about what a pleasure it was to work with you or your firm
- Narrated project case study with charts and photos – possibly with interviews of the client(s) and team members

There are many ways to incorporate video into your reputation building. Within the Power of the Podium section, I shared an example where I was required to video myself speaking in front of an audience, and then submit it for consideration to speak at a national conference. After recording it, I took a snippet of it and embedded it on my LinkedIn profile. Here I promote myself as a speaker, so it makes sense to provide a few examples.

One of my favorite examples of video use in this industry was actually uncovered by the "Three SoMegos" while writing a white paper for the Society for Marketing Professional Services Foundation. Holly Bolton, Dana Galvin-Lancour, and Adam Kilbourne partnered to write the white paper, and I had the pleasure to serve as a liaison between them and the publisher, the SMPS Foundation. Early on, they began referring to themselves as the "social media nerds." I didn't like the moniker – it didn't fit their personal brands! So I suggested a few alternative names, and the one that stuck was a combination of a movie title ("The Three Amigos") and the common abbreviation for social media (SoMe). The Three SoMegos were born! They authored *The Clients' Viewpoint on Social Networking and Media*, and included several case studies that they had found during their research. One related to eBay and their plans to construct a modular data center within an existing building in Phoenix. But there was a catch: the 8,000 sq. ft. data center had to be designed with maximum flexibility and scalability, able to handle an IT load of at least 4 megawatts. An RFP was issued through the Data Center Pulse blog and promoted to the blog's LinkedIn Group. The shortlisted firms were announced on

YouTube. The selection was also announced on YouTube, with the winning architect on video, participating in the conversation. It was an innovative process, and the architect was able to build his reputation as an expert in modular data centers through the conversations that played out on YouTube, which were viewed by several thousand people.

I've really just touched the surface of social media sites in this section. Google + is another growing social media site for people to network. Pinterest, Instagram, and Flickr allow people to post images and likes. About.me.com allows you to create a single location for all your social media links. Many people are using FourSquare to share their location at any given time.

Some organizations have also set up their own social networking sites, accessible only by active members of an organization. An example of this is MySMPS (www.mysmps.org), a community of the Society for Marketing Professional Services. There's also the Design & Construction Network (www.mydcn.com), which began as a LinkedIn Group and spread to its own, independent site. Here you can connect with more than 50,000 A/E/C professionals.

There's a world out there waiting to meet you – all you have to do is connect.

The Tools:

- Company website
- Personal website
- Company blog
- Personal blog
- LinkedIn
- Twitter
- Facebook
- About.me
- Google+

Reputation Design+Build

- YouTube
- Pinterest
- Instagram

Tools Part 2: Building Your Reputation

Case Study: Daniel Kerr, PE

Dan Kerr is president of Burns Mechanical in the greater Philadelphia region. It is a relatively new position for him as he previously served as Director of Energy Services for McClure Company. Both are mechanical contracting and engineering companies that are subsidiaries of PPL Energy Services. A mechanical engineer by training, Dan is passionate about green buildings and renewable energy – something that comes through to readers of his blog posts and prolific Tweets.

While with McClure Company he created a blog, The M Files, as a play on the popular television series The X-Files. While the slogan of that series was "The Truth is Out There," Dan's blog tagline was "The Truth is in Here." His blog homepage made it clear what The M Files is all about: "Hi! I'm Dan Kerr. Welcome to my blog, where I'll be sharing slightly countercultural views of energy, sustainability, and the construction industry." A blogger since 2009, Dan's goal with McClure was to author two blogs per month. His topics have included: "The 3 Problems with LEED Energy Goals," "3 Secrets of Recommissioning Older Buildings," and "Net-Zero Buildings: Legitimate Policy or Hallucination?" He's also racked up thousands of Tweets and gained several thousand Twitter followers in the process. Interestingly, his Twitter handle hints at another passion of his. The handle is @RunOnEnergy, and one of Dan's hobbies has been competing in the Iron Man Triathlon.

Although Dan will be the first to admit that the impact of social media on his reputation isn't always measurable, he does state: "My reputation is certainly strong, and social media definitely plays a role in that." According to Dan, "One tangible outcome is being asked to write a periodic guest column for the MidAtlantic BX on green building issues. Some national trade journals have also reached out to me about writing and a few of my posts have gained traction on reputable national and international sites." Interestingly,

Dan has found a side benefit from his efforts: "What I enjoy most is how employees internal to our own organization come to me for energy and green building advice. When your own troops are on board with your expertise, work life gets a lot more rewarding."

Dan takes great pride in how he helped position McClure Company as an industry leader and "voice of reality" in the region, although the personal brand he has developed has created some head-scratching opportunities: "I pride myself on engineering ability, so I find it a little odd to get asked to speak about brand building and social media to professional marketers. I've also done that several times." If you are interested in blogging, Dan still wants to be the "voice of reality": "Blogging is hard work. I'm naturally wired to write and still have trouble making the time to get it done." Yet, Dan also feels there are benefits to blogging beyond reputation-building: "I'm a believer in treating writing like exercise. The way to build writing 'muscle' is to write often. I'm a much better writer now than when I started blogging."

When he became president of Burns Mechanical in June 2013, his time for blogging naturally dwindled; however, he has since picked up where he left off, and now blogs monthly for Burns Mechanical. His posts have included such titles as "Distinguishing between energy use and energy cost," and "Innovation: Advanced high-performance building themes gleaned from AEI student competition." As for McClure's M Files blog, it lost its voice. More than two years after Dan's departure, the most recent post is the last one Dan wrote before he left.

Next Steps:

1. Create personal accounts on the primary social media websites: LinkedIn, Facebook, Twitter, Google+, and YouTube (even if you don't have anything to post right now).

2. Try to use the same name/handle for every website, because that helps with brand consistency.

3. Write multiple bios of yourself at varying lengths – a short one (140 characters) for Twitter, moderate length (200 words) for LinkedIn, and longer version for company or personal website.

4. Come up with a "headline" that captures who you are and what you do (see the Personal Brand Statement section of this book for more information).

5. Begin connecting with people you know on LinkedIn, and following people that interest you on Twitter.

6. Join applicable Groups on LinkedIn (e.g., organizations that you belong to, areas of interest).

7. Begin reading blogs related to your passions and industry – what are other professionals writing about?

8. Start a list of potential blog topics – it could be the same list you develop for potential articles.

Expanding Horizons: Pro-Bono & Freelance Work

Another way to enhance your reputation is by providing your services at reduced rates or even pro-bono to an organization in need. There are many professionals willing to do some upfront work gratis, using the approach as a loss-leader in the hopes of scoring a larger project if and when things move forward.

But the pool of professionals that will actually provide their services free of charge is smaller. The One Percent is an interesting organization that encourages design professionals to dedicate 1% of their annual hours to providing pro-bono work. Architectural firms small and large have joined the program, creating an avenue for non-profit organizations to access services that may otherwise be unavailable.

Pro-bono work can be very simple, like developing a cost estimate or reviewing drawings for a non-profit organization constructing a new building. Or it could actually involve providing free design for that project. One of my former colleagues has exceptional Revit skills. He started with creating basic renderings, but soon advanced to full-blown architectural renderings. When a non-profit organization was looking to bring entertainment to a local town square during Saturdays in the summer, he modeled the town square in Revit and then added artists, musicians, crowds, and even food trucks. The visuals were used at the public unveiling of the new programs and seen by hundreds of people in the audience.

When I built a personal brand as someone with extensive knowledge of local history and architecture, I got to know a number of elected and appointed officials in city government. It was the history/architecture background that served as an introduction, but when they found that I was a marketer by profession and had written visitors guides for the county tourism bureau, they began picking my brain on a variety of topics. Eventually, I offered to develop a tourism marketing plan for the downtown, which was implemented by the local Main Street organization. As part of the plan, I created a concept for a downtown-specific visitors guide, wrote the copy, and provided photos. We brought in a publisher and the guide became a reality. All my work was pro-bono. I was helping the city, the downtown merchants and restaurants, and the local Main Street organization – where I soon became a board member and officer. I did have the opportunity to do other work with the publisher as a paid freelancer.

I was able to utilize my professional skills and passions to help my community and a non-profit organization. What are your skills and who could benefit from them?

Professionals can also "moonlight" in one form or another. As defined by Tom Peters in his "Brand You" article in *Fast Company*, moonlighting is something that you do within your firm, going beyond your job description. While it is typical for a designer or estimator to move into project management, the moonlighting approach is more atypical – like helping with human resources management or information technology. The concept is to provide a service that is important to your firm and where there is a need, essentially going above and beyond the call of duty.

It could still be technically-related. Perhaps you are in a position that doesn't require construction estimating, but you volunteer to help the staff that does this function, adding depth to their department and gaining new skills. Or you work behind a desk, but there is a need for someone in the field. Volunteer to fill that void. Look at where your company has needs, and figure out where you can help alleviate them.

Why would you want to do this? First, it builds your brand within the firm, enhancing your relationships with co-workers. Second, it gives you new skills and an expanded knowledge base. Third, it makes you indispensable. The Great Recession taught us all that there are few indispensable employees — but if you are able to expand your role and assume new responsibilities, you've greatly increased the value you provide to the firm and differentiated yourself from your co-workers.

This will benefit you, both as you advance in your career and during times when your firm is evaluating downsizing options. Plus, it will make you more marketable if you look for employment elsewhere — sort of a design and construction utility player.

There may also be opportunities to enhance your reputation through an outside job. This is what most of us think of as moonlighting. I once met a professional services marketer who co-owned a restaurant. She spent her evenings and weekends as hostess and manager. Her network was very supportive of her outside venture, so members of the design and construction community often dined at the restaurant — after all, it was "one of their own" — and when design and construction conferences were held in town, attendees would regularly dine at the restaurant.

A friend of mine was a civil engineer by day, and then transformed into a landscaper during off-hours, building elaborate backyard gardens with water features. He used the same skills for both jobs, but they are also distinct from one another.

Some professionals are also involved with running family businesses on the side — or yes, even multi-level marketing companies.

It's not uncommon for certain professionals to work on the side and provide the exact same services they do on their day job, just in a non-competitive way. One of the most common examples of this is the architect that designs commercial or institutional projects by day, and then changes into a residential architect by night and weekend. Because his or her employer doesn't design single family homes, there is no competition — and the architect is gaining new skills while growing his or her network.

Hobbies may also be a source of side income. As a parent, you might be a volunteer coach for your child's sporting team. But these sporting leagues need and pay for umpires and referees.

While a few extra bucks are always nice, the side work you do – for free or for fee – builds your personal brand and expands your network.

The Tools:

- o Nonprofit organizations
- o Moonlighting within your firm
- o Family businesses
- o Non-competing freelance work
- o Hobbies

Reputation Design+Build

Case Study: The 1%

The 1% is a program that connects architectural and design firms with nonprofit organizations needing design assistance. Launched by Public Architecture, and inspired by the work of the Community Design Collaborative of the AIA Philadelphia and the Taproot Foundation, the organization asks firms to give 1% of their time, at no cost, to organizations in need.

Examples of completed projects include a new nursery school in San Francisco, an outdoor classroom in North Carolina, a children's library in Dallas, and a community center in Virginia.

As of this writing, the organization's website states that more than 419,000 hours are pledged annually, with 1380 architectural firms participating and more than 900 non-profits in need of assistance.

While some of the major firms like HOK, Gensler, Perkins+Will, and Cannon Design are involved with the program, so are countless smaller architectural and design firms who just want to do something meaningful for non-profit organizations in need.

Learn more at www.theonepercent.org.

Case Study: James Abell, FAIA

James Abell is committed to social responsibility through architecture. Every year, his small firm – Tempe, AZ based Abell & Associates Architects, Ltd. – undertakes a community project at a reduced fee or pro-bono arrangement. Some of their pro-bono projects have included the Casa Teresa Women's Shelter in Phoenix, Grampa Charlie's Healing Garden in Tempe, Harrison Square in Phoenix, and Lambert-Miller Art Gallery in Phoenix. James has been featured in the publication *Social Responsibility in Architecture* and was honored with the 2010 Edward C. Kemper Award for Service to the American Institute of Architects as well as the 2014 Thomas Jefferson Award for Public Architecture. According to an *AIArchitect This Week* article, "James Abell has time and time again been the public face of what architects and the AIA can do to help people in need of better cities, towns, neighborhoods, streets, homes, and businesses." He is a Fellow of the American Institute of Architects and also a Landscape Architect.

James is an active member of the American Institute of Architect's Regional/Urban Design Assistance Team (R/UDAT) Program, which has helped more than 150 communities across the United States become more livable. He first became involved with the program in 1974, and led his first national team in 1994, participating in more than 15 community design charrettes in several states. One of James' memorable R/UDAT experiences was helping Lancaster, Texas rebuild after a devastating tornado tore through town. Although it is his architectural background that brought him to these communities, much of what he does is bring people of diverse socio-economic backgrounds together in an effort to build or recapture civic pride.

James firmly believes that "Fairness and good citizenship is its own reward," and he has worked to instill that philosophy on the young architects and students. He says that many of them "Want to learn 'shortcuts,' yet I have tried patiently to prepare them for contributing mightily to their profession, their community, and their culture first, without having immediate or tangible benefit for themselves ... dollars are not the only way to be 'paid'."

As for the benefits of volunteerism, James believes that "The ripples you send across the pond mark your impact and that energy is returned in ways you can never know. I became a better public speaker every time I was challenged in a tense public meeting. I became a better person every time I was exposed to the hurt and loss some citizens were suffering from their tornado-devastated town. I never thought for a minute I was 'building a reputation,' but rather simply being an agent for 'building a better America!' And guess what? It made a better me!"

Next Steps:

    1. Research opportunities to get involved with an organization like The 1% or contact local nonprofits about pro-bono work.

    2. Look around your firm and determine if there are opportunities for you to "moonlight" and go above and beyond your job description.

    3. Consider freelance work on the side to gain new skills and expand your network.

    4. Delve deeper into your hobbies – is there a way to make them more "public"?

Embracing Your Creative Side

There are countless creative people in the design and construction industry. The demands of the profession – and increasingly budget-conscious clients requiring more with less when it comes to budgets and fees – require a high level of creativity.

These same skills are often employed for a creative outlet in the arts. After seeing your vision for a project or system sucked into the vacuum of cost-savings and value engineering, it's sometimes nice to be able to fully realize your creative vision.

I've met quite a few architects who are also artists. Sometimes they do the work as a quiet hobby, and very few people get to see their talents. Other times they share their paintings and sketches with larger audiences by exhibiting at local galleries or submitting their work for judged competitions.

Some professionals are also musicians on the side. Just looking around my own firm, some of my co-workers over the years have sung with the local symphony chorus, shared their vocal talents with their church choir, or rocked it out on weekends playing guitar at local clubs.

Photography is another natural outlet for design and construction professionals because photography is an everyday part of the job. And while most in the industry are just point-and-shoot photographers recording existing conditions or construction progress, some enhance their skills and develop a full-blown hobby. They join photography clubs, participate in exhibits at art galleries, and submit their work for contests and potential publication in magazines. Actually, photography is one of those moonlighting skills that can add a lot of value within your firm. Professional architectural photography is expensive because it is one of the most challenging of all photography disciplines. But if you have some skills at photographing buildings, sites, and bridges, you can save your firm money by bringing the service in-house, at least for the non-essential work.

Acting at the local community theater is another creative outlet for your talents. Interestingly, acting is a way to greatly enhance your public speaking skills and gain confidence in front of an audience. There are a number of industry consultants that come from the acting community and teach "show business" skills to design and construction professionals to help them in their daily jobs.

Re-enactors and living historians also fall within this category. A re-enactor dresses in period attire and "acts" as though they were a person from that period, usually in conjunction with a historical event or at a historic attraction. A living historian dresses in period attire but stays in the present day and discusses the person or period they are portraying (referred to as interpretation).

As a local historian, I have been involved with several historical organizations – which has led me to don period attire on multiple occasions. One of my hobbies for several years was to bring local Civil War history to the forefront. My hometown is located near Gettysburg and was the largest Northern town occupied by the Confederate Army during the Civil War. Town leaders negotiated with the advancing Army of Northern Virginia to spare the town from destruction, and thus the community has traditionally been tight-lipped and downplayed the history.

However, as I worked with others to accurately tell the story and establish the community as part of the Pennsylvania Civil War Trail, I increasingly found myself talking with executives of local companies who were supportive of my efforts. I also found myself dressed as a Union private, Confederate general, and Victorian townsperson. It was amazing to me to realize how many local business leaders had a strong interest in this history, and we found a connection through my participation as a living historian.

By the very nature of your job, you're a creative person. So what artistic endeavor awaits?

Tools Part 2: Building Your Reputation

The Tools:

- Painting
- Sculpture
- Art
- Music
- Photography
- Theater
- Re-Enacting

Reputation Design+Build

Case Study: Laurin McCracken, AIA, FSMPS

Laurin is an architect by training and currently serves as Chief Marketing Officer for Jacobs Global Building. Before earning a bachelor of architecture from Rice University and a master of architecture and urban planning from Princeton University, Laurin first earned a bachelor of arts from Rice. And while he has built his brand as one of the leading minds in professional services marketing – recognized as a Fellow of the Society for Marketing Professional Services and a past recipient of the prestigious Weld Coxe Marketing Achievement Award – he has also built a brand as one of the nation's leading watercolor artists.

Laurin's work hangs in corporate and private collections, including the industry-related collections of McGraw-Hill and the Urban Land Institute. His work has received many prestigious awards, from such exhibitions as the Louisiana Watercolor Society, Kentucky Watercolor Society, International Exhibition Watercolor Art Society, Tennessee Watercolor Society, Southern Watercolor Society, Texas Watercolor Society, and the list goes on. His work has also appeared in numerous publications, including *The Best of Watercolor, Watercolor, The Artist's Magazine, Watercolor Magic, American Artist,* and *Watercolor Artist,* among many others.

Another interesting fact about Laurin: he is a signature member of more than a dozen watercolor societies. How did he make a name for himself? According to Laurin, "My reputation was built in three actions: one, getting published; two, entering, getting accepted and winning awards in major state, region, national and international juried shows; and three, giving workshops." Although editors of art magazines and books now contact him for content, Laurin has continued to use his artistic skills to benefit his other profession. For instance, he donated a giclee print to the Society for Marketing Professional Services Foundation for a fundraising raffle. At their national convention, he took the stage to draw the winner and surprised everyone by offering a percentage of his revenues to the Foundation for his works purchased by SMPS members.

Today, Laurin wears two hats: marketer and artist. He has two signature lines for his emails – one with his business contact information and his AIA and FSMPS credentials, the second with AWS and NWS – the signature designations for the country's top two watercolor societies. He has proven that one can excel at two professions and be equally passionate about both.

Case Study: Christopher Brooks, LEED AP

Chris Brooks is a senior associate with Acoustic Distinctions, and former owner of his own firm, Orpheus Acoustics, an architectural acoustics consultant firm. His background includes consulting for performing arts centers, churches, and synagogues, meeting spaces, and other areas where noise control is required. Chris authored the book *Architectural Acoustics* and contributed to *The Integrative Design Guide to Green Building*. You might say that Chris lives acoustics, because he is also a professional musician. He plays the violin and viola and has performed with the Seville Symphony (Spain), Frysk Orkest (Netherlands), Harrisburg Symphony Orchestra (PA) and Lancaster Symphony Orchestra (PA).

His unique combination of passion and profession – music and acoustics – has created an interesting brand as Chris is both an end-user and consultant. According to him, he "regularly pulls out the professional musician card" at prospect meetings and client interviews, because it helps connect him with the clients and potential clients.

Furthermore, Chris feels that his artistic sensibility informs his profession, and he's excited when the two come together, as was the case when he was invited by the AIA Central PA and Society of Design to participate in a Pecha Kucha (Japanese for "chit chat"), where he married the violin to a story about performance and acoustics. He's also helped to inspire a generation of architectural engineering students at Drexel University, regularly presenting on acoustics and using his musical background to bring theory to life.

Chris continues to build his brand within both of his passions – acoustics and music. He's increasingly become a presenter, speaking about the relationship between architecture and acoustics as well as acoustics in health care environments. One of most interesting presentations he gave was at the Girard College Founders Hall, a National Historic Landmark in Philadelphia. Here he participated in a performance of "Awakened Ruins," and was able to talk about acoustics from the point-of-view of an artist. Chris is also working on his second book, a guide to improvisation for string players. If you talk with him about his passions, you're bound to be asked a simple but profound question designed to make you think: "Has the art of listening been lost?"

Next Steps:

1. Identify any artistic talents you may have or want to pursue (hint: you're never too old!).
2. If you enjoy acting, get involved at a local community theater.
3. If you enjoy photography, join a local camera club or submit your work to a regional publication.
4. If you are a musician, join a local group (e.g., chamber singers, orchestra, rock & roll band).
5. If you are an artist, join a local art association and submit your work for an exhibition.
6. If you are a re-enactor, offer your services (and uniform, and equipment) to a local historical organization.

Mentoring Your Replacement

"Tell me, and I forget, teach me and I may remember, involve me and I learn." Such were the words of Benjamin Franklin, and they apply to your responsibility as a mentor.

Did you have a mentor? Someone who *involved* you in their profession or approach? Someone whose wisdom made you a better person or professional? If you did have a mentor, you already know the value of having one. If you didn't have a mentor, you may subscribe to the "baptism by fire" approach and advocate self-study or trial and error as superior to having a mentor.

But the reality is that you personally gain a lot by mentoring. The process is as valuable to the mentor as it is to the mentee. Most people have a want to share knowledge in one form or another – writing, speaking, or mentoring. For those who work in a company environment, mentoring is a critical responsibility to share best practices and lessons learned with younger and less-experienced staff members.

Mentoring, however, is also a reputation-building tool. When you are willing to share knowledge gained throughout the course of your career, and help staff of all levels become more knowledgeable or skilled in a particular process or approach, you are demonstrating the importance of giving. You may be an example for your colleagues and a role model for the younger staff.

Mentoring can be accomplished in many ways. Larger firms have formal programs while smaller firms may have informal mentoring – that happens across a desk, conference table, or restaurant booth. You can mentor someone on a specific design or construction-related skill. Or how to manage a project or people. Or soft skills that a mentee will need as they advance in their career. Or information that will help a mentee pass a certification or licensure exam.

Professional associations often offer mentoring programs, and you can volunteer to participate and work with mentees one-on-one or in small groups.

There really are no restrictions on mentoring, other than you have to be offering information of value to the recipient. Mentoring is a two-way street, and if you or the mentee feel forced together, you'll probably have limited success and it won't be a positive experience for either of you.

If both parties are willing and dedicated, you may in fact be mentoring your replacement, be they a current employee or someone external to your firm. Most of us suffer from the "too much work, not enough time" disease. So while it is easy to spin that scenario into an excuse to avoid mentoring, the reality is that a better route to take is the "I'll make time because this is really important" approach. Mentoring someone can actually help alleviate some of your workload. And as for mentoring your replacement – that's a good thing because it will allow you to take on new responsibilities and advance in the organization.

I've heard concerns among potential mentors for external opportunities (e.g., mentoring for a professional association) that they are resistant to being involved because they might be teaching skills to someone who may become a competitor. That doesn't hold much water, because more often you'll be teaching skills to someone who will become a valuable friend and ally. Few people will actually use the advice you give them against you. But your knowledge, your helpful advice and encouragement, can make a real difference in someone's career. And no matter where each of you goes in your careers, they will always remember what you did for them.

Your mentee, or mentees, will become your advocates. As they advance through their careers, they may be in position to introduce you to new people who belong in your network, provide testimonials on your behalf, or even give work to you or your firm.

You get what you give, so you should be liberal when it comes to giving advice and sharing knowledge with up-and-coming professionals. Whether or not you subscribe to the concept of karma, giving in this manner will rarely not come back to you – and even if it doesn't, you are still a better person for helping to advance someone else's career.

The Tools:

- o   Formal program
- o   Informal training
- o   Professional organizations
- o   Lunches
- o   Lessons learned and stories

Tools Part 2: Building Your Reputation

Case Study: Adam Snavely

As president and CEO of The Poole and Kent Corporation, a Maryland-based mechanical contractor, Adam Snavely has been involved with multiple organizations. He has served as a board member of the Mechanical Contractors Association of America, president of the Mechanical Contractors Association of Maryland, and on the board of trustees of Contractors and Unions Together. He is also committed to mentoring, and has been able to enhance his brand and develop valuable relationships through his involvement with mentoring and training programs.

While serving as president of the Baltimore Chapter of the ACE Mentor Program, which he became involved with in 2006, Adam worked with a team to recruit new schools and new members to expand the program. He's made it a mission for his staff at The Poole and Kent Corporation to participate, and as part of the EMCOR Group has encouraged staff at other EMCOR companies to get involved. In fact, his company essentially "adopted" the Baltimore Chapter, providing financial support, human resources, and facilities. Adam enjoys going out to schools and giving presentations, because he feels that it is important to "find ways to help bring people into the industry." When he became president of the local chapter, he took the viewpoint of "If you are going to go, go big." To wit, his goal was to get people talking about ACE. Whereas the program's presentation night used to draw 50 people, it was soon drawing 300 people.

Adam's role as the organization's champion built his brand in the local community, and the marketing connection benefited his firm. His brand expanded nationally when he was featured in an ACE advertisement that ran in trade publications, and he also promoted ACE through a video on YouTube. Some of his former mentees interned with The Poole and Kent Corporation, and Adam regularly keeps in touch with many of the students he mentored. "I consider myself an industry person," Adam states, "I know that if I can do something to further this industry, it will ultimately benefit our company directly or indirectly." Because of that, Adam took his role on the board of directors for the Mechanical Contractors Association of America and focused on giving back to his profession by serving as a teacher and facilitator at the MCAA Institute for Project Management held at the University of Texas.

His dedication to mentoring and teaching opened another door for Adam when he was asked to serve on the board of directors for the Maryland Center for Construction Education and Innovation (MCCEI), a public-private partnership focused on providing career pathways in construction, collaborating with educational institutions, and integrating new technologies. Adam believes that, "You can't learn everything from a lecture hall, you have to have a mentor." By creating a culture of mentoring at Poole and Kent, dedicating countless hours to the ACE Mentor Program, teaching courses for MCAA, and helping to create a better tomorrow in Maryland's construction industry, he has elevated his profile and that of his company while at the same time doing much good for his profession and gaining valuable business relationships. To Adam, though, it's just another day at the office: "I believe a significant part of my daily responsibilities include some aspect of mentoring – that is part of leadership. That is my responsibility."

Next Steps:

1. Develop a knowledge sharing program for you and your co-workers to share lessons learned and personal experience with others within your firm.
2. Conduct a "gap analysis" within your firm, comparing senior and junior staff to determine which skills need to be passed on to younger staff.

3. Get involved with your company's mentoring program, or create a new program if one does not already exist.

4. Join the regional chapter of ACE and become a mentor.

5. Determine if your professional associations have mentoring programs; if they do, offer to become involved. If they don't, offer to start one.

Soccer Moms (& Dads) Bring Home the Bacon

The phrase "bring home the bacon," which refers to earning money, is believed to have originated in twelfth century England, where a custom emerged to give a young couple bacon if they were still together after a year of marriage. In the fifteenth century, European peasants would purchase pork only when special guests were coming for dinner because the meat was normally too expensive. By the late 1970s, commercials for the perfume Enjoli were capturing the trend of more women in the workforce, combining the archaic phrase with a catchy jingle that people still remember today: "I can bring home the bacon, fry it up in a pan, and never let you forget you're a man…"

Through all these centuries, the phrase has continually referred to getting something – bacon, pork, money. Thus the title for this section, because Soccer Moms and Dads alike can bring home the bacon when it comes to building their network and enhancing their reputation.

The point is that you never really know from where the next great contact or next business opportunity is going to come. My friend and colleague William Long, PE, LEED AP, FSMPS, is an ardent believer in this because he experienced it first-hand. He had been trying to gain an audience with an executive that he thought belonged in his network – and had the potential to give work to his firm; however, the traditional routes had proven unsuccessful. Then his son decided to become a Cub Scout, and Bill volunteered to be a leader. Imagine his surprise when he learned that the busy executive not only lived near him, but was also involved with the same Cub Scout pack! Before long, Bill found himself at the executive's house, planning Scouting activities and then getting to know

Tools Part 2: Building Your Reputation

one another better afterward. Years have passed, but this executive is still a friend and an important member of Bill's network.

If you have children, there are many benefits to becoming involved with their activities, whether coaching their sports team, helping to lead their Scout troop, or serving on their school's Parent Teacher Organization. Not only will you be helping your children, and getting to spend more time with them, but you will be meeting like-minded parents. Some of these parents may become part of your network – or may be able to introduce you to people they know who can help you or your company. This type of involvement certainly helps enhance your reputation as well, as you are showing leadership skills and a commitment to youth.

One of my co-workers was a soccer coach, and through his involvement over several years he got to know an executive with a local *Fortune 500* company. It turned out that this executive was in a position to hire our firm, and we ended up with literally millions of dollars of design work over the years with this single client. And all of that work can be traced directly to a youth soccer team!

Helping your children and their friends have fun and experience new things is an awesome feeling and a reward unto itself. But while you are focused on leading their teams or troops, be sure to look around and get to know the other parents. You never know who they are, what they do, or how they can help you unless you say hello and develop a relationship with them. Your involvement doesn't need to be formal – new friendships and business relationships can be made at children's birthday parties, play groups, or on the sidelines of sporting events.

The Tools:

- o   Parent teacher organizations
- o   Youth sports
- o   Youth activity groups

- Scouting
- Play groups
- Birthday parties

Next Steps:

1. When your children express an interest in an activity or organization, encourage them and determine how you can become involved.
2. Engage the other parents wherever you go – get to know them. As your friendships develop, determine if you can help them in any way. They will most likely reciprocate.
3. BUT – do not "stalk" people you want to meet by getting involved with their children's organizations – that's just creepy and inauthentic.

Networks Above, Below & Beside

Networking may seem like a redundant tool – after all, there have already been sections on joining community groups, professional associations, and client organizations. When you attend an event with other people – be it a meeting, trade show, or conference, you are networking. However, there is a difference between *networking*, the verb, and *network*, the noun.

Merriam-Webster defines networking, in a business sense, as "the exchange of information or services among individuals, groups, or institutions; *specifically*: the cultivation of productive relationships for employment or business."

Network, however, is defined by Merriam-Webster as "a usually informally interconnected group or association of persons (as friends or professional colleagues)."

Networking is getting to know a lot of people through many different means. Your network, on the other hand, is limited to those people that (1) you have a mutually-trusting relationship with, and (2) can benefit you or your company.

So while you may meet hundreds of people at networking events throughout the course of a year, you may decide that only ten – or two – of those people belong in your network. Here are some basic criteria for determining who should be in your network:

o Can they directly award work to you or your firm?
o Can the advocate for you to someone who can directly award work to you or your firm?
o Can they help get you in front of decision-makers through referrals, recommendations, setting up speaking or writing opportunities, getting you involved with their organizations, etc.?
o Are they up-and-coming, and have a bright future as a decision-maker even if they aren't now?

I've seen various statistics about how big one's network should be, and most fall within the 100-150 person range, though some recommendations go as high as 300 people. Think about that: do you currently have trusting relationships with 150 people that can benefit you or your company? You probably have more than you think – but you probably don't use this network to its fullest extent. Your network may include:

- Clients
- Former clients
- Vendors
- Co-workers (same office, different offices)
- Former co-workers
- Community leaders
- Business leaders
- Professional association contacts
- Client organization contacts (potential clients)
- A/E/C professionals (even competitors)
- College alumni
- Fellow country club members
- Golf league companions
- Personal friends
- Family
- Former members of your network that you've fallen out of touch with

In other words, the network "pool" is huge, so long as the candidates meet the two simple criteria: (1) a mutually-trusting relationship, and (2) can benefit you or your business.

Your network is a vital tool for building and maintaining your reputation, because many of the opportunities featured within the other tools require a current and vibrant network.

Do you know or work with someone who seems to know *everyone*? If you call and asked them a question, they seem to be within one or two degrees of separation of someone who could answer that question, and they could get you an answer quickly. That person has a robust network.

Pick up any book about network building, and you're apt to learn that the first rule of networking is giving – and not expecting anything in return (in the short-term). This is a significant point. How do you build trust? You demonstrate, through your actions, that you have value and can help someone.

Give information. Provide leads. Offer to make introductions. Think about how you could help someone in your network, and also keep your ears to the ground and eyes on the lookout for something that could benefit the members of your network.

If you are at a networking event, and realize during a conversation that the person you are speaking with doesn't have a place in your network, but could add value to someone else's network, offer to connect the two. Or if you glean a lead from a conversation, share it with the person in your network who could use it – or even recommend that person during your conversation with the lead-source.

There are obvious limitations – you certainly can't share information that was shared with you in confidence. And you can never use information received from someone against that person (e.g., sharing the information with their competitor).

As you become a valuable source of information and leads to members of your network, you will build trust with them. The payoff comes when they share information and leads with you.

With mutual trust, you develop a win-win situation where you are helping one another. And when you have 150 key people in your network, there is a lot of helping to be spread around. But it does require maintenance.

If you don't maintain your network – staying in regular contact with each and every person in it and continually adding value – than your network will wither like an un-watered flower.

Your network will also require regular pruning. Are there people in it that no longer belong there? Perhaps they have changed positions or careers. Maybe they never reciprocate, and you feel that you've given enough without getting anything of value in return. That's okay. Move on – it doesn't mean that you can't still be friends or maintain contact with that person, but move them out of your network so you can move someone else into it – someone that could provide greater value.

When you are the recipient of giving from a member of your network, be sure to reach out and thank that person. A personal "thank you" – handwritten note card, email, or phone call – goes a long way. Don't feel like you have to immediately reciprocate, but just continue to add value to your relationship whenever possible.

Part of your success at building and maintaining this network will be your ability to recognize whenever you come across something that could be of value to a member of your network. This may be a full-blown lead (for a project, for a new job), information about one of their clients or prospects, an opportunity for them to speak or write, an introduction that would help expand their network, or even a simple gesture like forwarding an article that may be of interest to them.

You'll need to keep track of your network. By that I mean that (1) you always need to know where members of your network are, so follow them whenever they switch jobs, and (2) you need to begin compiling a database of useful information about them. This could include their birthday, college, spouse's name, children's names, hobbies, sports, etc. When they open up and share something personal about themselves with you, make a note of it because it may come in handy in the future.

Tools Part 2: Building Your Reputation

Harvey McKay, a best-selling business author, created the "McKay 66" as a way to track customer knowledge; however, his list of 66 items you should know about them is equally applicable to members of your network. You can find a copy online at http://www.harveymackay.com/pdfs/mackay66.pdf.

If you don't already know – with certainty – who is in your network, make a list, and keep track of it. You can use handwritten notes, a dedicated CRM program (Vision and Cosential are popular in our industry, ACT is a very popular contact tracking and CRM option), or Microsoft Outlook. Make a note of every conversation or communication – email, telephone, meeting, event – and any pertinent information discussed. Add personal details. Make a note of what you gave – or what you received. Reference this list continually, and set up contact reminders if you are using CRM software.

Our memories fail us often, and it is difficult enough to remember a conversation we had last week, much less a conversation we had two years ago! So make these notes as soon after your conversation as possible. If you were at an event and had a lot of conversations with different people, your mind will tend to blur the discussions, and soon you won't remember who told you what, which is all the more reason to document the conversations immediately after they occur.

This will provide a treasure trove of data about the members of your network, and also serve as a reminder of your giving and receiving activities.

William Dillard, founder of Dillard's Department Store, famously quoted "Location Location Location" when asked about the secret to the store's success.

To paraphrase Mr. Dillard and apply his quote to reputation building and management, the secret to success is "Network Network Network!"

The Tools:

- Co-workers and former co-workers
- Vendors
- A/E/C industry colleagues and organizations
- Local business community
- Client organizations
- Friends
- Family
- Volunteer efforts
- Social networking

Next Steps:

1. Understand that "networking" actually means "giving."
2. Create and maintain a CRM database of all the people you meet – use a special field or code to designate those who belong in your network.
3. Select 100-150 people to be in your network – people who can help your career, direct business to your firm, or connect you to others.
4. Share articles, information, and leads with members of your network – but expect nothing in return (if you give, you will get).
5. Reach out to members of your network at least four times annually – through a face-to-face meeting, phone call, personal email, letter, or handwritten note. In-person meetings are always best, as are conversations with them more than once a quarter.
6. Always help members of your network, even if they don't ask for it.

Tools Part 2: Building Your Reputation

7. Refresh your network often – if members don't provide value or never reciprocate on the giving, replace them.

References & Testimonials

Despite all the excellent tools available to help you build your brand and enhance your reputation, few things are more important than references and testimonials. These offer proof that you are as good as your brand promise. You can obtain advanced degrees, write numerous articles for publication, speak at client events, and regularly attend networking events. However, if others don't hold you in high regard, than those other tools will never succeed. When others respect you and think you provide value, they are apt to recommend you.

Research conducted by Hinge Marketing in their publication, *VISIBLE EXPERTS: How High Visibility Expertise Helps Professionals, Their Firms and Their Clients*, verifies this. More than 1000 clients were surveyed, and they overwhelming stated that recommendations from friends and colleagues convinced them, more than anything else, that someone is an expert. In fact, more than 56% of survey respondents chose this option, far ahead of a person's track record (experience), published articles, presentations, or online presence, among others.

This was also echoed by research conducted by the SMPS Foundation that found that when companies look for A/E/C firms or professionals, they often turn to their peers for recommendations. And once they have candidates, they look at references or testimonials to verify they are making the correct decision in hiring the individual, team, or firm.

As demonstrated earlier in this book, owners are increasingly requiring personal references for each member of the project team – often instead of references for the firm(s) pursuing the project. Just think about this tectonic shift. Instead of marketing departments listing three or four company references as part of a proposal, they now must list three or four references for each member of the project team: architects, engineers, project managers, construction managers, specialty consultants, quality reviewers, surveyors, site superintendents, estimators, and the list goes on.

Now think about your own background. Do you have three good references that will speak to your performance on their projects? What about three references for each of the market segments that your company pursues? The thought can be daunting, particularly if you are not "front line" staff. While the project manager and construction manager are regularly in front of clients during the life of a project, often times the other design and construction positions are only present when their discipline is required, if at all. Furthermore, many project team members, who handle the bulk of the design production or construction work, never even meet the clients. So how can they possibly have owner references?

What does this mean? It is imperative that you build a personal brand and become known among your clients – you need them to help you and your firm get the next project!

The thing about personal references and testimonials is that they must always be current. A reference about a project that you worked on 20 years ago won't cut it. In fact, just as a lot of clients want three example projects completed in the past three years, or five projects in the past five years, your references should follow a similar approach. So if you work for a design or construction firm that does a lot of institutional work, you may need to have 3–5 educational references and 3–5 health care references. Furthermore, if the educational work your firm pursues includes both higher ed and K–12, you'll need several references for each. If you are being proposed as a project manager or executive, the references should be relevant to your role – and not references for being a project engineer or site superintendent.

In addition to project references, you should always have business and personal references. These could be people you've worked with through your involvement with professional associations or community organizations. If you plan to submit to be a speaker at a meeting or conference, be prepared to have to include three references who have previously heard you speak. This is why it is often good to start small, speaking to local audiences, be they from chapters of professional associations or service clubs like Rotary International. With these you rarely need speaking references to get the gig, but once you've spoken a few times – and of course done an excellent job! – you'll have several potential references to use.

Company marketing departments are regularly in pursuit of client testimonials – reference letters, quotes for marketing collateral, or even videos. Often when clients provide quotes, they single out specific project team members. Make sure you know when your name is being mentioned, and get copies! These quotes are great for resumes and can help enhance your brand. Likewise, if an unsolicited letter or email gets sent to the project manager or an executive, and you are mentioned, make sure that you get a copy for your records.

Even when you aren't specifically singled out, if projects you worked on receive positive remarks from the clients, get copies. If a client is quoted in the media talking about how awesome the project is – even if you or even your firm is not mentioned by name – obtain a copy. You can always include that quote with a project description on a resume. While you won't be able to broadcast that quote to the world, you may be able to link to it on your social media channels. A simple, "Honored to have been project engineer for [project name]; so glad the client is pleased!" Include a link to the article if it is online.

Speaking of social media, this is where your LinkedIn profile can be an excellent venue for showcasing your talents. Although you will be able to complete almost all of the LinkedIn sections on your own, the Recommendations section relies on others to provide the content. This is where your connections can write glowingly of your capabilities and their experiences working with you. You don't need to have dozens of these, but you should have several to complete your LinkedIn profile. Do clients, or potential employers, actually read these? Look no further than the case study at the conclusion of this section. Josh Carney started his firm during the height of the Great Recession. Fortunately, he had a number of happy clients (architects and owners) that had positive experiences working with him. When asked, they were pleased to write a short testimonial on Josh's behalf. He credits these LinkedIn Recommendations with establishing immediate credibility for his fledging firm.

Don't be afraid to ask people to write testimonials on LinkedIn, but give them some guidance. Reach out to them and ask if they would be willing to write something positive about their experience working with you on a certain project, or with a certain organization. Or perhaps they heard you present and can write about the impact of your presentation and speaking skills. Maybe they can address your thought leadership, or your involvement with the profession or industry. Often they will not only agree to write a Recommendation, but will actually ask you what to put in it! Focus on a key point or two that reinforces the personal brand that you are looking to portray. If you provide input into multiple Recommendations, be sure to make them different from one another, even if they are focused on a similar theme.

But remember, this is a two–way street. Offer to write a testimonial on their behalf – or just do it. Do you want to make a person's day? Write a meaningful, honest, and unsolicited LinkedIn Recommendation for someone you know and respect. Imagine their delight when they receive a notification that you have done that for them! They are likely to offer to reciprocate, so take them up on it. Or maybe they really don't care about a testimonial from you, but there's another way you can help them – making an introduction, recommending them to speak or write, helping them to find a new job, or something else.

The Recommendations your connections write for LinkedIn – or in a letter or email – will be critical to providing the proof that your brand is real, and the brand promise that you have created by using the various tools is, in fact, true.

The Tools:

- Referrals
- Testimonial letters
- Testimonial videos
- Social networking endorsements
- Achievements and awards

Tools Part 2: Building Your Reputation

Case Study: Josh Carney, PE

Josh Carney is at an interesting place in his career. Experienced enough to lead his own structural engineering firm, Carney Engineering Group, young enough to stay abreast of the latest technology trends. Although he opened his firm during The Great Recession, he was able to grow it steadily through the turbulent economy because of his brand of providing value through not just his structural engineering, but also by being focused on his customers.

If you visit Josh's LinkedIn profile, you'll find a series of recommendations from satisfied clients. "Josh has become a trusted partner on many, many projects." "He has a knack for customer services and is always focused and determined to find the right solutions for each client." "...(I) have always found him to have a thorough expertise, dependable, personable, punctual, and highly creative." "He brings exceptional value to his clients via a strong expertise in structural engineering design coupled with his skillful management of personnel and resources." These are some of the comments that Josh's happy customers have posted on LinkedIn – for the world to see.

Josh has some great advice for anyone who wants a testimonial or reference for themselves or their firm: ask for it. "I am always amazed how hesitant we are as an industry to ask people to do this," he says. Josh has been proactive in asking for feedback, and he did so by asking his clients to answer a specific question: "At the end of the day, what I asked the people who wrote those (references) to do was tell me why they worked with me instead of all the other options they have. I have my own opinions why people come to us, but wanted to get outside views that would speak to the concerns our clients would have."

In additional to the personal recommendations, Josh has also posted some firm references on his company website. Because Josh Carney's personal brand is directly tied to the brand of Carney Engineering Group, it was the testimonials that helped make a difference during the difficult early days of starting a new company from scratch, in the midst of a recession: "While I was somewhat known in the industry, we certainly struggled to be taken seriously when we started up. The testimonials enabled us to establish a certain credibility with new prospects that I am not sure we could have developed any other way. On multiple occasions, I have been told how people researching us have been surprised at the testimonials, and have commented they gave us a try on the basis of what was said."

Next Steps:

1. Contact five clients and ask for referrals or testimonial letters.
2. Ghostwrite testimonial letters for clients – combining their "voice" with key points that will be of interest to potential clients (or future employers).
3. Ask a client to provide a testimonial about you or your firm on camera – draft a short script for them (then take them to lunch afterward!).
4. Reach out to LinkedIn connections who have worked with you – either as a client or a colleague – and ask them to write Recommendations for you on LinkedIn (and also offer to reciprocate).

Knowledge

It is one of the most overused phrases of the English language, and yet holds as true today as the first time it was uttered: "Knowledge is power."

Have you ever talked with someone who seemed to know everything about everything? Not a gossip, but one who could engage in intelligent discussions on a seemingly endless array of topics? Although we may occasionally come across one of these people who leaves us with the less-than-stellar impression as a "know-it-all," most people who fit this category impress us and even leave us with a bit of envy: "How can they possibly know all this?"

The various tools discussed in this book all require a level of knowledge. While it might seem obvious for the thought-leading tools of writing, speaking, and public relations, as well as the degrees, licenses and certifications, you need to have a vast mental database of knowledge to make you a great conversationalist. This is important whether you are meeting with a long-term client or stepping out of your comfort zone and into a networking event for the first time. There's nothing worse than having nothing to say or add to a conversation. So how do you gain knowledge?

Read. Attend. Watch.

I'm always amazed when I talk with a senior-level person who doesn't read their local newspaper. I used to think that *everyone* read their local newspaper, but that seems to be less and less the norm. Even if you work internationally, it is important to stay abreast of the news in your hometown. What's the local political scene like? What companies are moving to the area or laying off? What is the community talking about – a major fire or scandal (yes, it is gossip – but printed gossip!)? The local newspaper provides a rich amount of content and, as a result, unlimited conversation starters.

Regional business journals are also excellent sources of information – they typically cover a larger geographic area and are targeted to business professionals. Here you can keep track of local economic trends, companies, and other business professionals. They publish lists about everything. Yet how widely are these periodicals distributed within your firm? In a lot of design and construction firms, they may never go beyond the executive office or the marketing department. They also often end up in the company lobby. If your company doesn't receive the regional business journal, subscribe. And if it does, make sure your name is added to the circulation list.

National newspapers like the *New York Times*, *Wall Street Journal*, *Washington Post*, and *USA Today* provide excellent sources of information about international and national events and business news, and have robust content available online for free. Business-focused magazines like *Business Week*, *Fast Company*, *Fortune*, *Forbes*, and *Entrepreneur* also offer a lot of free content on their websites or apps, so you won't be starved for information or go broke in the process of gaining it!

As mentioned in the Education section, A/E/C industry publications are another excellent way to gain knowledge. From reading periodicals specific to your discipline to more general industry publications like *Engineering News-Record* or *Building Design + Construction* to those that focus on non-technical skills, you'll be more well-rounded if you eagerly devour this type of information. While a structural engineer reading *Civil + Structural Engineer* is a pretty easy correlation, that same structural engineer reading PSMJ's *Project Management* or Zweig Group's *Zweig Letter* is not so obvious. Yet these publications can provide valuable knowledge to the structural engineer, helping him or her to become a project manager or enhance their skills, while also gaining a better understanding of how firms develop business in this industry.

In business development, one of the keys to success is to demonstrate that you understand your clients' (or potential clients') industry. Know the challenges they face and what issues keep them

Tools Part 2: Building Your Reputation

awake at night. Know their trends and their competitors. Know how to speak their unique language. This knowledge is often easily gained by reading the publications that your clients read. Often, you may be able to get a free subscription. Or simply identify the publications, and visit their websites regularly. You may be able to read the entire magazine, or at least select articles.

Another excellent, and often affordable, knowledge tool is the webinar. Most organizations, along with myriad private corporations, regularly offer webinars. Some are free, others cost one hundred to a few hundred dollars. Some even award continuing education units that can help you reach your re-licensing or re-certification requirements. Once again, think big-picture here. Don't just sit through webinars directly-related to your core job function. Sit through the webinars your supervisors and clients are sitting through. I've attended some excellent webinars and some that weren't really worth the money. However, I almost always take away a nugget or two of information that can be useful in my job or conversations. Of course, this sometimes includes, "I just spent $300 on this webinar and overpaid by $299!"

Professional associations provide valuable continual learning opportunities to their members, in the form of publications, webinars, and regular chapter meetings. These meetings actually provide a double-dose of brand-building because they allow you to gain knowledge while also expanding your network – or getting to establish deeper relationships with other members who regularly attend the meetings. I've known many competent professionals who have paid their membership dues year-after-year to belong to an organization, but never actually attended any meetings. This represents wasted money and missed opportunity.

Most organizations, whether they cater to the design and construction industry or to the clients we serve, hold conferences. For some, there is one annual national conference. Others may hold an annual national conference as well as a series of regional or topic-specific conferences. These represent another excellent opportunity to grow your knowledge base (and your network). As you build your reputation using the tools in this book, you may eventually decide to submit an abstract to speak at one or more of these conferences. But whether you are a presenter or not, you can gain a deeper understanding of certain topics, learn new industry trends, gain competitive intelligence, and better understand your clients. The first step is to attend conferences specific to your discipline or function, like an architect attending the AIA National Convention or a contractor attending the Associated General Contractors Annual Convention. Next are the more overarching conferences that attract a broad cross-section of the A/E/C industry. Examples of this would be ENR's FutureTech Conference, PSMJ's Industry Summit, and the Greenbuild International Conference and Expo, presented by the U.S. Green Building Council. Finally, there are the conferences that your clients attend, like the Construction Owners Association of America's Spring and Fall Owners Leadership Conferences or APPA's annual Conference and Exposition. Attendance at these client-focused conferences increases your knowledge of your clients' issues, allows you to expand your network, and creates opportunities for new business development.

Trade shows are often conducted in conjunction with regional and national conferences, but are frequently the main attraction itself. There are most likely trade shows related directly to your profession, and here you can learn about new products and processes while networking with colleagues and vendors. But there are also trade shows targeted specifically toward your clients, and once again these shows provide the opportunity to better understand your clients and their industries, while also allowing for new business development. Examples include the Process Expo of the Food Processing Suppliers Association and National Restaurant Association Show – both of which are in the Top 40 largest trade shows in the United States. Of course, local business associations

Tools Part 2: Building Your Reputation

(like chambers of commerce) typically hold annual expos, and here you can network with local businesspeople and – if your practice is smaller and locally-based – perhaps interface with clients.

Podcasts are growing in popularity, so much so that iTunes now has iTunes University, where you can download lectures from colleges across the country. Some professional and client associations offer podcasts, or audio recordings of presentations, at no or nominal cost to members. Download one to your mobile phone or iPod, and then listen when you're on the go and further expand your knowledge base.

We are living in the so-called Knowledge Era (although that phrase is not universally accepted), which succeeded the Information Age. To most of us, we are actually in the Information-Overload Age. We can't keep up with email, websites, magazines, podcasts, social networks, television, and our day jobs! So how can we satisfy our thirst for knowledge without drowning in it? Google has created a tool for this, and it is known as Google Alerts. Simply surf to www.google.com/alerts and enter specific words or phrases that you want to monitor. Google will send you regular emails with links to sites that have those words and phrases. I also have keywords set up in Google News, so every time I scroll through the main News page, there are specific, relevant links to certain categories of news that I track.

The Tools:

- Local newspapers
- Regional business journals
- A/E/C industry publications
- Client industry publications
- Webinars
- Society and association meetings
- Regional and national conferences

- Trade shows
- Podcasts
- Google Alerts & News

Next Steps:

1. Subscribe to a local business journal(s) or ask to be placed on routing list of the office copy.
2. Regularly visit websites of national and business media, including *New York Times*, *Washington Post*, *USA Today*, *Wall Street Journal*, *Business Week*, and others. Read articles to expand knowledge base and identify trends that may impact your clients and their industries or the A/E/C industry.
3. Subscribe to *Engineering News-Record* and regularly visit ENR.com for industry news and trends.
4. Subscribe to other industry publications like *Building Design + Construction* or discipline-specific periodicals like *Civil + Structural Engineer*.
5. Read the publications of the professional associations to which you belong and/or ask to be placed on the routing list for other professional association publications.
6. Visit websites of client organizations like COAA, IFMA, ASHE, ULI, and others; read their free content to help determine what trends are driving their businesses or institutions.
7. Subscribe to client publications, or visit their websites for free content.
8. Subscribe to publications of FMI, PSMJ Resources, or Zweig Group to learn more about the management and marketing side of the A/E/C industry and identify applicable trends.

9. Attend trade shows targeting your clients to learn about trends and products.
10. Attend A/E/C industry conferences to learn about trends, best practices, and gain competitive intelligence.
11. Attend webinars targeting A/E/C firms or client industries.
12. Subscribe to blogs or podcasts targeting A/E/C firms or client industries.
13. Set up Google Alerts for certain keywords so salient news and links are regularly sent to your email.

Additional Tools

One of the most important tools you can create is your resume. The marketing department of your firm may have a professional resume used for marketing the firm and including within proposals. Depending upon the complexity of the marketing program, it may be automated and capture every project to which you've ever charged time. More likely, there is always a mad scramble to update your resume with relevant projects every time a proposal is submitted to a potential client.

When the marketing department maintains your resume, it is convenient because very little work is required on your part. However, you *own* your resume – your company or marketing department does not. You should be the one continually updating it – and not just with descriptions of projects you designed or constructed.

As covered earlier, your portfolio is a key tool – one that can help your firm land projects and help you gain new employment. Your education, licenses, and certifications are an important component of your reputation. Your professional association, community group, and client organization involvement is a component of your personal brand. The same holds true with articles and blogs you've written and presentations you've given.

Not only do you need to be doing several of these activities, but you also need to be keeping a record of everything that you've done. Under the Virtual Reality section, we covered the LinkedIn profile, and how it parallels the various reputation-building tools. This is the data you need to be tracking, but in even more detail. Never rely on your memory, and instead assume that at any moment in time you may need to have access to your past activities and successes. The worst-case scenario is that you'll find yourself unexpectedly looking for a new employer. More likely, you'll use this information for completing social media profiles, personal awards submissions, bios for board of directors nominations, and other activities.

Your personal resume should include far more information than you will ever give out at any single time; however, it must be robust and include *everything*. Don't just list the projects you worked on with short descriptions. Include your project role(s), challenges, and how you (and/or the team) overcame the challenges. List any unique experiences (was it your first BSL-3 project or first Revit design?). Who were your client contacts? Who were the other team members – both colleagues and other firms including architects, engineers, specialty consultants, contractors, etc.? If the client wrote a testimonial at project completion, include that – whether or not you were singled out by name. Did the project win any awards? List those, too. The purpose here is to provide a high level of detail about each project, because you never know when you are going to need the information. Here's an example of required project information, taken directly from a Request For Proposal:

- o Project title
- o Occupants/tenants/clients
- o Location of the project
- o Date of contract award
- o Date of substantial completion
- o Construction cost at award
- o Construction cost at completion
- o Scheduled completion time in days
- o Actual completion time in days
- o Number of change orders
- o Scope of project including design, permitting, construction, construction administration, approval process by local/state/federal regulatory agencies
- o Special features
- o Images of completed project – interior and exterior

- Two references for each completed project including client name, email, phone number, address

That's asking for a lot of information, but some RFPs require even more, like:

- Original design schedule
- Actual design schedule
- Reason for any delays
- Original construction schedule
- Actual construction schedule
- Reason for any delays
- Number and cost of change orders during *design* phase
- Reason for change orders
- Number and cost of change orders during *construction* phase
- Reason for change orders

Including any degrees you've obtained is obvious, but listing all your continuing education is not. However, you should. Include educational conferences attended, bootcamps held by organizations like PSMJ and Zweig Group, Dale Carnegie and Toastmasters training, industry-specific programs, leadership training, and anything else. Again, you most likely won't list this information in its entirety whenever you create a resume, but it is good information to track. Include dates of completion and source of training.

You'll also want to include information about your organizational involvement, be it community groups, professional associations, or client organizations. List everything you were involved with, and the respective dates. What was your role: volunteer, committee member, committee chair, board of directors, and/or officer? If you had multiple roles, list each and every one, and the dates of service. What were your accomplishments or unique experiences?

Likewise, you should track your writing and speaking endeavors. For writing, include title, name of publication, and date of publication. Include articles for the company newsletter or blog, professional association publications (chapter, regional, or national level), local periodicals like newspapers and business journals, books or chapters of books, client or industry publications, and any other writing credentials of note. It's also a good practice to save copies of all your published works, and scan any print publications to build a digital portfolio of your clips.

For speaking, list the organization or audience, including presentations to college classes. Presentations at company lunch-n-learns or to community and service groups should also be included. The dates of presentations and short descriptions about each topic are also important. If speaker scores were provided, be sure to maintain a copy for your records, and list your best scores and audience comments on your personal resume. Also, if you receive any positive feedback afterward, in the form of a note or email, capture the comments and add them to your master resume.

Awards and honors is another category to include, whether the recognition was project-related or personal. Even the smaller honors, like a speaking award from a Dale Carnegie program, should also be listed.

Ultimately, the purpose of this personal resume is a *database of your career*. If your firm has a marketing department, they would love a copy, but this resume should also reside on your personal computer (and in hard copy) in your home. This is all about you and your accomplishments, and whenever you need to submit a resume – for a personal award or when you are a candidate for election to a board of directors – you'll have a master to pull from. Plus, in the event you are ever "downsized," you will already be a step ahead of the game when it comes to getting a resume together for potential job opportunities.

Another tool is the "Personal Brand Statement," a somewhat abstract phrase, but really just a quick overview of who you are. Think of it as an elevator speech about yourself.

I believe that there are three elevator speeches. The first and most effective is only four words: "Tell me about yourself." There are books and even classes dedicated to helping you prepare your elevator speech, but regardless of whether you are talking about yourself or your company, the main point here is that *you* are the one talking, not the other person.

Whether in business development or reputation building, it is always wise when meeting someone new to find out about them first. So ask them – give them the opening to share their elevator speech. In business development terms, this can help you prequalify whether or not there is any opportunity for your firm. In reputation building and management, allowing the other person to talk about themselves will help you determine whether or not they should be in your network and if they could possibly benefit your career.

That stated, there are also times when someone will beat you to the punch, and ask you to go first. You'll have to determine if you need to give your *company* elevator speech or your *personal* elevator speech. If you are at a conference or convention, the other person, or people, may actually help you decide. They will look at your nametag and the company listed on it, and ask about the company. That makes it easier, although it is always a good idea to first identify yourself and your role. For instance, "Hi, Scott Butcher, vice president of JDB Engineering. We're an engineering firm focused on client success through project innovation for manufacturing, life sciences, and food processing companies."

There are a lot of consultants, and business books, out there, that want you to use an elevator speech with a value statement tied to it. That approach has several problems, first and foremost the fact that if you are meeting someone new and thus know nothing about them, how could you possibly offer to them value without even knowing their needs? The second problem, and I've experienced this countless times, is that these value-proposition elevator speeches sound rehearsed and often don't tell the recipient a thing about who you are or what you do. Steve Jobs, founder of Apple and one of the greatest business presenters of our time, believed that "simplicity is the ultimate sophistication." What a great way of looking at things!

The third type of elevator speech is your personal brand statement, or whatever you want to call it. Essentially, this is the fifteen- or thirty-second commercial about you. I like to compare it to Twitter or LinkedIn headlines. It should cover who you are and what you do. "Hi, Scott Butcher. I'm vice president of JDB Engineering and oversee the sales and marketing functions. I've also been known to dabble in writing, photography, and history." Compare that short statement to my LinkedIn headline: "Scott Butcher, FSMPS, CPSM. VP of JDB Engineering, author of 10+ books, marketer of professional services, photographer, Fellow of SMPS." The two statements – the more conversational one that I might use to introduce myself, and the more formal written one on LinkedIn – don't need to be identical, but they should be similar and thus reinforce one another.

You should always have a few business cards with you. I find it amusing that some personal branding gurus recommend that you have your own personal business cards with your own personal logo. If you are self-employed, then of course this makes sense. But having multiple "identities" can be very confusing to the recipient of the card, especially if you are at an event where you are wearing a nametag and the company listed does not match your business card. Use your company business card! Remember, the process of building your reputation has a correlation in building your firm's brand. Name, company, telephone, email – those are the basics. Most corporate business cards also list titles, address, website, and appropriate post-nominal letters (PE, AIA, LEED AP). Business cards are still an important part of the business world, but increasingly most people will look you up online after you meet in person. In fact, if you connect with someone on LinkedIn or another social networking site, programs like Microsoft Outlook can pull their contact information directly into your Contacts database. Likewise, smartphones with social media apps can pull the contact information directly onto your phone.

The Tools:

- "Personal Brand Statement"
- Professional resume
- Personal resume
- Business card

Next Steps:

1. Update or create a comprehensive resume with the following:
    a. Work experience and responsibilities
    b. Projects including challenges, solutions, and relevant data
    c. Education
    d. Continuing education including conferences
    e. Community organization participation and responsibilities
    f. Professional association involvement and responsibilities
    g. Client society participation and responsibilities
    h. Articles/blogs written including publishers and dates
    i. Speaking engagements including organizations/audiences and dates

Tools Part 2: Building Your Reputation

       j. Awards and honors received including personal and project-related
       k. References and testimonials.
2. Provide a copy of your comprehensive resume to your firm's marketing department. They will thank you.
3. Continually update your master resume with current information.
4. Develop and memorize your personal brand statement and company "elevator" speech. Prepare different versions (short and long).
5. Practice asking questions of others to get them to open up to you and deliver their own personal brand statement or elevator speech.

Combining the Tools

Design and construction professionals who have built their brands know that the most effective way to create their reputations, and maintain them once established, is to use multiple tools. Getting involved with community groups and professional associations builds your network. The same professional association that builds your network may publish an article you wrote in their newsletter. And that article, in turn, may create an opportunity to speak about the topic.

You don't need to use every tool available. Actually, you shouldn't use every tool, because it will be too overwhelming and you may not be effective as you'll be spreading yourself too thin. The last thing you want as a brand attribute is "underperformer."

As evidenced in the case studies throughout this book, successful professionals have figured out how to utilize a few tools exceptionally well, building positive reputations and differentiating themselves from others in their field. Several of the case studies came about from a few simple Google searches! If I'm searching for an engineer with an advanced education, or an architect with a deep portfolio of speaking experience, and your name comes up first, then you are at the top of a category.

Other case studies came about by asking colleagues to identify co-workers who fit specific profiles. If a co-worker immediately thinks about you when I ask for an example of a construction professional who advanced his or her career through publishing or social media, then you've built a powerful brand within your company.

Several years ago I attended Build Business, the national conference of the Society for Marketing Professional Services. It had been a decade since I had last attended one of these conferences, and I received a lot of value from it. While there, I had the opportunity to moderate three roundtables during one of the pre-conference

Tools Part 2: Building Your Reputation

activities, and on the train ride home after the conference, I started thinking about attending the next Build Business. But my company had paid a lot of money to send me to the conference, and I didn't feel comfortable asking to attend again unless I had a really good reason.

Or a discount.

I began thinking about how I could present at the next conference. When the Call for Presentations was announced, I delved into it, looking at each of the conference themes in depth. I evaluated each theme, as well as the proposed topics within each theme, to determine what matched my areas of expertise.

I came up with the idea of creating a presentation about personal branding. For two decades I had been working with my coworkers to position them as experts – no different than what thousands of other professional services marketers do daily – but I approached it from a "what about us?" perspective, as in "what about marketers and business developers?" I made an outline for a presentation, including the various tools that people can use for personal branding. Then I set about to find examples – case studies – to use during the presentation. A short online survey was created, and I used social media to invite SMPS members to participate. Additionally, I reached out to my network and asked for recommendations.

A lot of amazing people stepped forward and offered information and recommendations to inform the presentation.

After submitting for the conference, I sent out a few emails to regional chapters inquiring if they would be interested in having me present. Shortly thereafter, my home chapter asked me to give the presentation as part of a morning-long forum. Because I knew that shortlisted Build Business presenters might be required to submit videos, I recorded my presentation.

Fortunately, my presentation was short-listed, I was asked to submit a video, and eventually selected to present.

A few weeks later I received a surprise email from a marketing professional working to plan a regional SMPS conference in Texas. She had remembered my survey/request for case studies when I was researching the presentation, and asked if I had developed anything. That contact led to an invite to speak at a regional conference in Texas. On the heels of that offer, I made plans to vacation with family in Arizona the month following the Texas conference, and sent an email to the program chair of SMPS Arizona. After a few email exchanges they asked me to present while I was in the state, even rescheduling a presenter that had originally been scheduled for the week that I was in town.

As the national conference drew closer, the editor of *The Marketer*, the publication of SMPS, contacted me and asked me to write an article about my presentation topic for a special conference issue the organization was planning. I previously had three articles published in *The Marketer*, but it had been several years since my last article appeared in the publication.

And then Build Business rolled around. The presentation I had developed originally for the conference – "Beyond Marketing: Developing Your Brand as a Leader in Your Firm and Community" – had now been given three times already. These presentations, coupled with the feedback from evaluations and a few conversations with attendees, helped me edit and improve "Beyond Marketing" before the national conference.

Later, another opportunity presented itself via social media, when the organizer of a different regional conference posted a Tweet asking for presenter recommendations. Fortunately my name was suggested by a few SMPS members, and I followed up with the organizer and submitted an application that was accepted.

My involvement on the board of the local chapter of another organization led to an opportunity to repurpose the content into an article about personal branding for architects, published in the chapter newsletter (and on my company's website).

That article was an eye-opener for me, and I began to think about the concept of personal branding for design and construction professionals. I approached my friend Bill Long about my concept for a book and presentation on the topic. A colleague of mine, Adam Kilbourne, who I had worked with on a white paper (he was a co-author, I helped coordinate it for the publisher, the SMPS Foundation), contacted me about another regional SMPS conference. He had previously attended the "Beyond Marketing" presentation, and I shared that as an option as well as one about the concept I had discussed with Bill Long. Adam recommended the latter concept, and with Bill I submitted an application to speak at the conference in Cleveland. I wanted to bring Bill into the presentation because it was all about reputation building and management for technical professionals — and he was a licensed technical professional that had built an exceptional brand for himself. Talk about credibility! Our proposal was accepted.

As I began thinking about the presentation, I decided to create a version specifically for my co-workers, and presented it as a lunch-n-learn. Most of what I presented ended up in the reputation management presentation that Bill and I gave at the SMPS regional presentation. We took the show on the road, and were selected to present on the subject at AIA Philadelphia's annual Design on the Delaware conference as well as a SMPS national webinar. This was followed by selection to speak at the national conferences of the Associated General Contractors, Society for Design Administration, and Society for Marketing Professional Services, as well as other opportunities, like writing an article for a national publication.

This presentation was actually the spark that turned the idea for this book into a blaze. I had been researching and presenting on the topic for almost three years, and the book began flowing from my fingertips a few days after I returned home from one of the national conference presentations. The content from the original

Reputation Design+Build

"Beyond Marketing" presentation, as well as the personal branding for technical professionals lunch-n-learn I presented to my co-workers provided the majority of the content for this book!

So the initial concept and research led to:

- One presentation at a national conference of a professional association
- Two presentations to local chapters of a professional association
- Two presentations at regional conferences of a professional association
- One article in a national publication
- One article in a local chapter professional association publication
- One blog post on the company website
- One "repurposed" presentation at a company lunch-n-learn
- One "repurposed" presentation for local chapter of a professional association (co-presented)
- One "repurposed" presentation at a regional conference of a professional association (co-presented)
- Three "repurposed" presentations at national conferences of professional associations (co-presented)
- One "repurposed" presentation to a regional A/E/C industry conference (co-presented)
- One national webinar of "repurposed" content (co-presented)
- One article about "repurposed" content in national publication (co-written)
- One TED Talk-style presentation (second "repurposing" of content) to local chapter of professional association
- One book

Tools Part 2: Building Your Reputation

The original content looked at reputation and personal branding from the perspective of a marketer or business developer. The "re-purposed" content looked at it from the viewpoint of the technical professional, or even the marketer tasked with building the reputations of technical professionals. The second repurposing looked at the concept from an executive standpoint.

As they say, this topic "had legs." Great legs, in fact.

Case Study: Ardra Zinkon, IALD, MIES, LEED Green Associate

Ardra Zinkon has traveled an interesting route to become president of Tec Studio Inc., a Columbus, Ohio-based firm specializing in lighting and technology design. Whereas many lighting designers in the A/E/C industry come from electrical or architectural engineering backgrounds, Ardra earned a Bachelor of Arts in Theatre from Ohio State University, with an emphasis on lighting design. With this background, she began working as a lighting designer for a theater before moving to a consulting firm that specialized in lighting design. Later she joined Tec Inc. Engineering & Design, becoming both Director of Lighting Design and Director of the firm's Columbus office.

During this time Ardra was able to build an impressive personal brand by using many of the tools found in this book. She became involved with her professional associations, the International Association of Lighting Designers (IALD) and Illuminating Engineering Society (IES). Beyond merely attending meetings, Ardra served as an officer with the organizations' local chapters, and became involved with national committees as well. Through product reviews and publishing, she gained new knowledge while also enhancing her reputation by being listed in the national technical reports and presenting this information at association events. She says, "I think it has clearly built my reputation as a designer that knows technology, someone that can dig into the technical details to best support their clients' projects." More recently, Ardra was elected to the IES National Board of Directors, further solidifying her reputation as a leader among her peers.

Ardra also became involved with the Energy and Sustainability Committee of IALD and represented her profession in Washington, DC through meetings with members of the House and Senate Energy Commerce Committee, where she discussed lighting legislation. "Having a strong knowledge of the energy issues and upcoming legislation has also helped set us apart as a leader in the industry. My work on this committee led to several regional speaking engagements on lighting, green laws, and codes." Her speaking didn't stop there, though, as she has presented at major conferences including NeoCon, NeoCon East, Lightfair, IALD Enlighten Americas, and more. But becoming a national-caliber presenter isn't easy: "Speaking at a national level took a tremendous amount of work. Not just in research, but presentation skills and writing skills. I spent several years presenting first at the local and regional level before I finally got an opportunity to speak nationally. It's these types of challenges that we create for ourselves that I think really strengthen our skills overall, and again, all of that trickles down to our clients."

A certified LEED Green Associate, Ardra is passionate about the environmental impacts of buildings, and she has focused her efforts toward thinking about the sustainability of the systems she designs. This commitment gained her national recognition in 2010 and again in 2012 when she was awarded the GE Edison Award for Excellence in Environmental Design. The 2010 award was for her involvement in the Miami University of Ohio Farmer School of Business, while the 2012 award recognized her efforts for the new Hilton Convention Center Hotel in Columbus, OH. Her portfolio is filled with award-winning projects, including several that have been certified by the Leadership in Energy and Environmental Design (LEED) program. This impressive portfolio has also garnered Ardra status as the only professional member of the International Association of Lighting Designers in the state of Ohio.

Reputation Design+Build

Case Study: William Long, PE, LEED AP, FSMPS

It is difficult to write a short case study about Bill Long, as he has managed to effectively use pretty much all of the tools outlined in *Reputation Design+Build*! He has continually relied upon education as a means to further his career, originally attending The Pennsylvania State University and earning a bachelor of architectural engineering. His first job out of college was as a structural engineer with a Philadelphia-based design firm. Early in his career, Bill realized that he had a genuine interest in the non-technical aspects of the design profession and he returned to college, eventually earning a master of business administration from Villanova University. He transitioned into sales and marketing, and later attended courses from the Center for Management Research, a program taught by professors from Harvard University and Massachusetts Institute of Technology.

Bill's first professional license was as a Professional Engineer in the civil discipline. This was later supplemented by certification as a LEED Accredited Professional as well as the designation of Certified Professional Services Marketer (CPSM) through the Society for Marketing Professional Services (SMPS).

In the community, Bill served on the board of directors for the Pennsylvania Economy League for four years, and spent time as both a committee member and adult leader in Boy Scouting as his sons were active with Cub Scouts and Boy Scouts. He's also given back to his alma mater, serving on the Penn State Alumni Society of Architectural Engineers and dedicating time to both the communications/marketing committee as well as the outreach/continuing education committee.

As he became increasingly involved with business development and marketing, Bill found that SMPS offered a way for him to not only continue his education, but also become a leader in the organization. He served as president of the Philadelphia Chapter of

SMPS, then spent a stint on the national Board of Directors. Several years later he returned to national service when he was elected Trustee of the SMPS Foundation, where he went on to serve as president. He's been involved with the Delaware Valley Green Building Council, General Building Contractors Association, National Society of Professional Engineers, and other professional associations. Bill has also been active with a number of client organizations as a member, including Society for College and University Planning, Urban Land Institute, and American Society for Healthcare Engineering. He also served on the board of directors for the Delaware Valley Chapter of the International Society for Pharmaceutical Engineering.

An accomplished writer, Bill further established his brand by authoring articles for the SMPS *Marketer*, *Principal's Report*, *A/E Rainmaker*, and *New York Construction*. He researched and wrote a white paper for the SMPS Foundation, *International Success in the A/E/C World*, and wrote the *TRINIUM Resource Book, Higher Education Series* when he was a consultant and principal of TRINIUM Resources Group. Bill also wrote a regular blog, *The Flying Buttress: The Business Guide for the A/E/C Industry*. He authored a regular column for the SMPS *Connections* newsletter and has guest blogged on the Penn State Student Society of Architectural Engineering website.

Perhaps one of the things that Bill is best known for is his prolific public speaking. Whether at the local, regional, or national level, he's built an impressive list of speaking engagements for such organizations as the American Institute of Architects, Associated General Contractors, Construction Specifications Institute, American Society of Landscape Architects, Construction Management Association of America, International Society for Pharmaceutical Engineering, Society for Design Administration, and Society for Marketing Professional Services. He's also led webinars for SMPS, TRINIUM, and Axium.

With all these accomplishments it's hard to believe that he's had time for anything else. But he's managed to squeeze in formal mentoring for Philadelphia SMPS members working toward professional certification as well as students in Penn State's Architectural Engineering program looking to apply classroom knowledge to real-world realities. He's also been a mentor to many of the professionals that have worked for him during his career, whether he was helping technical staff transition to business development roles, or working with marketing staff to advance their careers.

For all his efforts, Bill was chosen to become a Fellow of the Society for Marketing Professional Services, one of less than 120 people in the United States to be awarded this designation, which recognizes only those with the highest level of experience and leadership in marketing and business development within the design and construction industry. He's twice been awarded the Cracked Bell Award by the Philadelphia Chapter of SMPS. Recently Bill was invited to join the Carpenters Company of Philadelphia, an exclusive organization of architects, contractors, and structural engineers with direct ties to the builders of Independence Hall. Today the organization invites professionals who have distinguished themselves through innovation in design and technical achievement.

Gap Analysis & Personal Marketing Plan

Much of this book is devoted to the various tools available to build and maintain your reputation. This next tool, however, will help you determine the next steps to take.

One important thing to understand is that you shouldn't look at the reputation management tools and think that you need to include something for each and every one of the tool categories. As evidenced in the case studies, most professionals who are having success with these tools are using more than one; however, few are using all of them.

Some people simply don't feel comfortable speaking in front of an audience. It is a great tool that can help you get far in your career, and I'd never advocate completely avoiding it. However, it is okay to put public speaking on the back burner and concentrate on another thought leadership tool like writing. As you build up your writing portfolio, you will actually have more to speak about, and have greater credibility to organizations seeking speakers. So focus on one or two of the tools to get started.

I know a lot of professionals that have trouble with the concept of networking, much less taking action. They are terrified to be in a room of strangers. Most accomplished networkers will tell you that *everyone*, themselves included, is uncomfortable at these events – and those that tell you that they aren't a bit uncomfortable are lying. That stated, some people have more of a knack for meeting new people and engaging in conversation than others do. So if you aren't involved with any organizations, become active with a local community organization or the local chapter of a professional association. You'll find yourself surrounded by like-minded individuals, and a few may even be your neighbors or co-workers. Worry about the client organizations down the road, once you feel more comfortable in a social/networking environment.

The tool that you can use to help determine the next steps for building your reputation is known as a Gap Analysis. A very simple definition is "a technique for determining the steps to be taken in moving from a current state to a desired future state" (www.businessdictionary.com). In other words, this is where you are now, this is where you are going, and these are the directions to get there – much like a marketing plan is created to move a corporation from Point A to Point B, raising visibility, building brand, and meeting revenue goals in the process. A Gap Analysis is your map. The tables on the following pages will help direct you as you complete your own personal Gap Analysis, and provide a roadmap for your reputation building and management activities. I'm referring to it as a Gap Analysis & Marketing Plan because not only will the questions help you identify your gaps, but they will also put you on the path toward filling those gaps, which actually means that you will be creating an action-oriented marketing plan. This information will also be useful as you develop or expand your comprehensive personal resume.

Gap Analysis & Personal Marketing Plan

Before we get into the Gap Analysis & Personal Marketing Plan, I want to acknowledge Bill Long for his contribution to this section. I developed a personal marketing plan for my co-workers, and he came up with a gap analysis for our presentations. I've married the two here.

Education & Training

College degrees that I currently possess	Date Earned
Bachelor:	
Master:	
Doctorate:	
College degrees that would benefit my professional status or reputation	Target Date
Bachelor:	
Master:	
Doctorate:	
Specialty Program:	
A/E/C workshops & bootcamps that I've attended	Date Attended
1.	
2.	
3.	
A/E/C workshops & bootcamps that would benefit me	Target Date
1.	
2.	
3.	
Professional association conferences that I've attended	Date Attended
1.	
2.	
3.	
Professional association conferences that I should attend	Target Date
1.	
2.	
3.	
Client & industry-related conferences and trade shows I've attended	Date Attended
1.	
2.	
3.	

Gap Analysis & Personal Marketing Plan

Client & industry-related conferences and trade shows I should attend	Target Date
1.	
2.	
3.	

A/E/C publications that I currently read
1.
2.
3.

A/E/C publications that I should read	Target Date
1.	
2.	
3.	

Client and industry publications that I currently read
1.
2.
3.

Client and industry publications that I should read	Target Date
1.	
2.	
3.	

A/E/C, client, and industry books that I've read
1.
2.
3.

A/E/C, client, and industry books that I should read	Target Date
1.	
2.	
3.	

Newspapers and business journals that I read
1.
2.
3.

Newspapers and business journals that I should read	Target Date
1.	
2.	
3.	

Blogs that I currently read
1.
2.
3.

Blogs that I should read	Target Date
1.	
2.	
3.	

CEUs required for re-licensing or re-certification	Date Required
1.	
2.	
3.	

Licenses & Certifications

Professional licenses that I currently posses	Renewal Date
1.	
2.	
3.	

Professional licenses that would benefit my career or enhance my expertise	Target Date
1.	
2.	
3.	

Required training for license renewal	Target Date
1.	
2.	
3.	

Certifications that I currently posses	Renewal Date
1.	
2.	
3.	

Certifications that would benefit my career or enhance my expertise	Target Date
1.	
2.	
3.	

Required training for certification renewal	Target Date
1.	
2.	
3.	

Portfolio Tools

In what project roles do I currently serve?	Years of Experience
1.	
2.	
3.	
In what project roles would I like to grow?	**Target Date**
1.	
2.	
3.	
What types of projects do I currently work on?	**Years of Experience**
1.	
2.	
3.	
What are my three greatest project accomplishments?	**Year**
1.	
2.	
3.	
What types of projects would I like to work on?	**Target Date**
1.	
2.	
3.	
What projects have I worked on that won awards?	**Award**
1.	
2.	
3.	
What personal awards have I won?	**Program/ Organization**
1.	
2.	
3.	

What projects have I worked on that should be submitted for awards? 1. 2. 3.	Program/ Organization
What personal awards could enhance my reputation? (Include Fellowships) 1. 2. 3.	Program/ Organization

Reputation Design+Build

Community Trusteeship

What are my top three passions, work-related or outside of work? Work/Personal
1.
2.
3.

What non-profit organizations directly relate to these passions?
1.
2.
3.

How could I directly impact the success of these organizations?
- ☐ Serving at the board level
- ☐ Serving on committees
- ☐ Providing design or construction expertise
- ☐ Serving as a loaned executive
- ☐ Training staff

How can I help these organizations raise funds to further their mission?
- ☐ Serving as account manager
- ☐ Conducting fundraising calls and visits
- ☐ Planning fundraising events for the organization

What local business organizations could benefit from someone with my skills?
- ☐ Chamber of Commerce
- ☐ Economic Development Organization
- ☐ Main Street Organization

Which service groups should I join? When?
- ☐ Rotary International
- ☐ Sertoma
- ☐ Kiwanis Club
- ☐ Lions Club
- ☐ Other:

Professional Associations

To which professional associations do I currently belong?	Level of activity

1.
2.
3.

Which professional associations should I join to enhance my expertise and network?	Target Date

Association:
  ☐ Local/regional chapter
Association:
  ☐ Local/regional chapter
Association:
  ☐ Local/regional chapter

What is my planned level of involvement for each organization (current or future)?	Target Date

Association:
  ☐ Attending meetings
  ☐ Serving on committees
  ☐ Becoming a director or trustee
  ☐ Serving as an officer or board president
Association:
  ☐ Attending meetings
  ☐ Serving on committees
  ☐ Becoming a director or trustee
  ☐ Serving as an officer or board president
Association:
  ☐ Attending meetings
  ☐ Serving on committees
  ☐ Becoming a director or trustee
  ☐ Serving as an officer or board president

Client Organizations

To which client organizations do I currently belong?	Level of activity

    1.
    2.
    3.

Which client organizations should I join to enhance my expertise and expand my network?	Target Date

    Organization:
        ☐ Local/regional chapter
    Organization:
        ☐ Local/regional chapter
    Organization:
        ☐ Local/regional chapter

What is my planned level of involvement for each organization (current or future)?	Target Date

    Organization:
        ☐ Attending meetings
        ☐ Serving on committees
        ☐ Becoming a director or trustee
        ☐ Serving as an officer or board president
    Organization:
        ☐ Attending meetings
        ☐ Serving on committees
        ☐ Becoming a director or trustee
        ☐ Serving as an officer or board president
    Organization:
        ☐ Attending meetings
        ☐ Serving on committees
        ☐ Becoming a director or trustee
        ☐ Serving as an officer or board president

Writing & Publishing	
What are some topics for which I have knowledge to share?	Level of Expertise

    Company or service-related topics:
        Topic 1:
        Topic 2:
    Client or industry-related topics:
        Topic 1:
        Topic 2:
    Personal interest or hobby-related topics:
        Topic 1:
        Topic 2:

What publications should I target for these topics?	Target Date

    Company publications:
        ☐ Blog
        ☐ Newsletter
    Local/regional media:
        1.
        2.
    Professional association publications:
        1.
        2.
    Client or industry publications:
        1.
        2.
    Personal interest or hobby publications:
        1.
        2.

If I wrote a book, what would I write about?
    1.
    2.
    3.

Reputation Design+Build

Presentations & Public Speaking

What topics am I qualified to speak about? (This list may parallel the writing list)	Level of Expertise

    Company or service-related topics:
        Topic 1:
        Topic 2:
    Client or industry-related topics:
        Topic 1:
        Topic 2:
    Personal interest or hobby-related topics:
        Topic 1:
        Topic 2:

What audiences should I target for these presentations?	Target Date

    Internal (company) audiences:
        ☐ Brown bag/lunch-n-learn
        ☐ Satellite office(s)
    Specific clients or prospective clients:
        1.
        2.
    Business organizations:
        1.
        2.
    Professional associations:
        1.
        2.
    Client or industry organizations:
        1.
        2.

Public Relations & Thought Leadership

With which media outlets do I have contacts?
   1.
   2.
   3.

| With which media outlets could I offer my services as an expert? | Target Date |

   Local/regional media:
      1.
      2.
   Professional association media:
      1.
      2.
   Client or industry media:
      1.
      2.
   Personal interest or hobby-related media:
      1.
      2.

What are the areas of expertise that I'm willing to discuss with the media?
   1.
   2.
   3.

| In what ways can I further develop my reputation as a thought leader? | Target Date |

   ☐ Conduct primary research & publish
      findings
      Topic:
   ☐ Author a white paper on topic of relevance
      to my profession or clients
      Topic:
   ☐ Develop a detailed case study about a
      unique or innovative project with which I
      was involved
      Project:

Reputation Design+Build

| Which marketing activities can help me establish my reputation as a thought leader? | Target Date |

- ☐ Press releases
- ☐ Postcards
- ☐ Fact sheets & backgrounders

Internet & Social Media

Which social media platforms will best allow me to interact with clients, peers, and community contacts?	Target Date

- ☐ Company blog: ☐ Currently active ☐ Will participate
- ☐ Personal blog: ☐ Currently active ☐ Will participate
- ☐ LinkedIn: ☐ Currently active ☐ Will join
- ☐ Twitter: ☐ Currently active ☐ Will join
- ☐ Facebook: ☐ Currently active ☐ Will join
- ☐ YouTube: ☐ Currently active ☐ Will join

What steps do I need to take to build or enhance my online presence?	Target Date

- ☐ Obtain professional photograph of myself
- ☐ Write short headline or profile for social media websites
- ☐ Write 200-word bio for use on social media websites
- ☐ Write longer 500-word bio for company website and other online uses
- ☐ Add social media links to my email signature

How can I expand my LinkedIn network?	Target Date

- ☐ Complete my Profile
- ☐ Connect with more colleagues
- ☐ Connect with more clients
- ☐ Join Groups – including organizations I belong to and areas of interest
- ☐ Post questions and comments to Group discussions and LinkedIn Questions
- ☐ Ask colleagues and clients for LinkedIn Recommendations
- ☐ Write LinkedIn Recommendations for colleagues and clients

Pro-Bono & Freelance Work

What skills do I have that could be used outside of my firm (management, design, construction)?
    1.
    2.
    3.

If I provided pro bono work to an organization in need, what type of services would I provide?
    1.
    2.
    3.

What organizations should I target to offer my services?   Target Date
    1.
    2.
    3.

What work opportunities and activities are there for me outside of my profession?
    ☐ Family business
    ☐ Hobbies/interests
    ☐ Other:

Which ways can I "moonlight" within my firm by going beyond my job description?   Target Date
    ☐ Cross-discipline training
    ☐ Estimating
    ☐ Site/Field Work
    ☐ Human Resources
    ☐ Marketing
    ☐ Business Development
    ☐ Information Technology
    ☐ Training & Development
    ☐ Other:

Arts & Culture

What are some creative outlets that I enjoy?
- ☐ Painting, drawing, sculpture
- ☐ Photography
- ☐ Music
- ☐ Acting
- ☐ Crafts
- ☐ Other:

At what venues or through which media can I showcase my creative talents?

1.
2.
3.

Mentoring

Does my firm have a formal mentoring program?
- ☐ Yes
  - ☐ Do I participate in it? ☐ Should I?
- ☐ No

If I created a mentoring program for my firm, what would it include?
- ☐ Mentor-Mentee matching
- ☐ Regular meetings between mentor/mentee
- ☐ External activities like quarterly lunches
- ☐ Knowledge sharing through articles/intranet
- ☐ Knowledge sharing through brown bag presentations

What opportunities are there for me to get involved with mentoring outside of my firm? Target Date
- ☐ Conducting/participating in license or certification study classes
- ☐ Leading training for professional, technical, or business organizations
- ☐ Joining ACE
- ☐ Participating in mentoring programs hosted by my professional association(s)
- ☐ Guest lecturing at colleges or high schools
- ☐ Other:

Networking

How many contacts do I currently have in my "network"? How many should I have?
    Existing:
    Target:

Which Customer Relationship Management System(s) do I currently use?
- ☐ None
- ☐ Paper files
- ☐ Outlook
- ☐ Act!
- ☐ Deltek Vision
- ☐ Cosential
- ☐ Other:

Which Customer Relationship Management System(s) should I use?   Target Date
- ☐ None
- ☐ Paper files
- ☐ Outlook
- ☐ Act!
- ☐ Deltek Vision
- ☐ Cosential
- ☐ Other:

How can I better help the people in my network?
- ☐ Share leads
- ☐ Make introductions
- ☐ Mail/email articles and information of interest, notes, etc.
- ☐ Provide free training in my area of expertise to them or their staff
- ☐ Help their family and friends
- ☐ Find out more about their businesses and needs
- ☐ Write recommendations or testimonials for them, even when unsolicited
- ☐ Ask for introductions or referrals

How can I expand my network?

- ☐ Maintain contact with existing clients
- ☐ Contact former clients
- ☐ Contact former co-workers
- ☐ Contact people I went to school with
- ☐ Meet regularly with vendors
- ☐ Attend professional association meetings regularly
- ☐ Attend client organization meetings regularly
- ☐ Attend conferences and trade shows
- ☐ Join a lead group
- ☐ Join a business organization or service club
- ☐ Make cold calls
- ☐ Give presentations
- ☐ Use social networking sites like LinkedIn
- ☐ Ask clients for referrals – who do they know?
- ☐ Other:

Who are the ten people that I absolutely need to have in my network?	Where can I meet them?
1.	
2.	
3.	
4.	
5.	
6.	
7.	
8.	
9.	
10.	

Referrals & Testimonials

Which of my existing clients do I feel comfortable asking for a referral?	Target Date
1. 2. 3.	
Which of my existing clients do I feel comfortable asking to write a testimonial letter about me or my firm?	Target Date
1. 2. 3.	
To whom am I connected with via social media that I could ask to write a recommendation about me?	Target Date
1. 2. 3.	
To whom am I connected with via social media that I could offer to write a recommendation on their behalf?	Target Date
1. 2. 3.	

Appendix – Links of Interest

Organizations & Societies

AACE International - http://www.aacei.org/

Academy of Geo-Professionals - http://www.geoprofessionals.org/

American Academy of Environmental Engineers and Scientists - http://www.aaees.org/

American Association of Museums - http://www.aam-us.org/

American Board of Industrial Hygiene - http://www.abih.org/

American Concrete Institute - http://www.concrete.org/

American Consulting Engineers Council - http://www.acec.org/

American Institute of Architects - http://www.aia.org/

American Institute of Constructors - http://www.professionalconstructor.org/

American Jails Association - http://www.aja.org/

American Planning Association - http://www.planning.org/

American Public Works Association - http://www.apwa.net/

American Resort Development Association - http://www.arda.org/

American Road & Transportation Builders Association - http://www.artba.org/

American Society for Healthcare Engineering - http://www.ashe.org/

American Society of Civil Engineers - http://www.asce.org/

American Society of Highway Engineers - http://www.highwayengineers.org/

American Society of Interior Designers - http://www.asid.org/

American Society of Landscape Architects - http://www.asla.org/

American Society of Professional Estimators - http://www.aspenational.org/

American Subcontractors Association - https://www.asaonline.com

Assisted Living Federation of America - http://www.alfa.org/

Associated Builders & Contractors - http://www.abc.org/

Associated General Contractors of America - http://www.agc.org/

Associated Specialty Contractors - http://www.assoc-spec-con.org/

Association for Facilities Engineering - http://www.afe.org/

Association for Preservation Technology - http://www.apti.org/

Association of Heating, Refrigerating, and Air Conditioning Engineers - http://www.ashrae.org/

Association of Physical Plant Administrators - http://www.appa.org/

BICSI - https://www.bicsi.org/

Building Owners and Managers Association International - http://www.boma.org/

Construction Financial Management Association - http://www.cfma.org/

Construction Management Association of America - http://cmaanet.org/

Construction Owners Association of America - http://www.coaa.org/

Construction Specifications Institute - http://www.csinet.org/

Construction Writers Association - http://www.constructionwriters.org/

Council of Educational Facilities Planners International - http://www.cefpi.org/

Design-Build Institute of America - http://www.dbia.org/

Illuminating Engineering Society - http://ies.org/

Institute of Electrical and Electronics Engineers - http://www.ieee.org/

Institute of Hazardous Materials Management - http://www.ihmm.org/

Institute of Real Estate Management - http://www.irem.org/

International Cost Engineering Council - http://www.icoste.org/

International Facilities Management Association - http://www.ifma.org/

International Interior Design Association - http://www.iida.org/

NAIOP Commercial Real Estate Development Association - http://www.naiop.org/

National Association of Home Builders - http://www.nahb.com/

National Association of Women in Construction - http://www.nawic.org

National Contract Management Association - http://www.ncmahq.org/

National Council for Interior Design Qualification - http://www.ncidq.org/

National Council of Architectural Registration Boards - http://www.ncarb.org/

National Council of Structural Engineers Associations - http://www.ncsea.com/

Appendix – Links of Interest

National Insulation Association - http://www.insulation.org/

National League of Cities - http://www.nlc.org/

National Registry of Environmental Professionals - http://www.nrep.org/

National Society of Professional Engineers - http://www.nspe.org/index.html

National Trust for Historic Preservation - http://www.preservationnation.org/

Precast Prestressed Concrete Institute - http://www.pci.org/

Professional Construction Estimators Association of America - http://www.pcea.org/

Project Management Institute - http://www.pmi.org/

Retail Contractors Association - http://www.retailcontractors.org/

Society for College and University Planning - http://www.scup.org/page/index

Society for Marketing Professional Services - http://www.smps.org

Society of American Military Engineers - http://www.same.org/

Society of Architectural Historians - http://www.sah.org/

Society of Cost Estimating & Analysis - http://www.sceaonline.org/

Urban Land Institute - http://www.uli.org/

US Green Building Council - http://www.usgbc.org/

Service Groups

Rotary International - www.rotary.org

Sertoma - http://www.sertoma.org/

Lions Club - www.lionsclub.org

Kiwanis International - www.kiwanis.org

Appendix – Links of Interest

Industry Publications

American School & University - http://schooldesigns.com/

American School Board Journal - http://www.asbj.com/

Architect Magazine - http://www.architectmagazine.com/

Architectural Record - http://archrecord.construction.com/

Area Development - http://www.areadevelopment.com/

Building Design + Construction - http://www.bdcnetwork.com/

Building Operating Management - http://www.facilitiesnet.com/bom/default.asp

Buildings - http://www.buildings.com/

Consulting-Specifying Engineer - http://www.csemag.com/

Contract - http://www.contractdesign.com/contract/index.shtml

Contractor Magazine - http://contractormag.com/

Control Engineering - http://www.controleng.com/

Corrections Today - http://www.corrections.com/

Engineered Systems - http://www.esmagazine.com/

Engineering News-Record - http://enr.construction.com/

Facilities & Destinations - http://www.facilitiesonline.com/

Facility Care - http://www.facilitycare.com/

Facility City - http://www.busfac.com/

Food Engineering Magazine - http://www.foodengineeringmag.com/

Food Processing Magazine - http://www.foodprocessing.com/

Food Service Equipment & Supplies - http://www.fesmag.com/

Grounds Maintenance - http://www.grounds-mag.com/

Health Facilities Management - http://www.hfmmagazine.com/

Hospitality Design - http://www.hospitalitydesign.com/

Hotels Magazine - http://www.hotelsmag.com/

Industrial Maintenance & Plant Operations - http://www.impomag.com/

Industry Week - http://www.industryweek.com/

Interior Design - http://www.interiordesign.net/

Library Journal - http://www.ljdigital.com/

Lodging Hospitality - http://lhonline.com/

Manufacturing & Technology News - http://www.manufacturingnews.com/

Manufacturing Automation - http://www.automationmag.com/

Manufacturing Net - http://www.manufacturing.net/

Material Handling Product News - http://www.mhpn.com/

Medical Design Technology - http://www.mdtmag.com/

Metal Architecture | Metal Construction - http://www.moderntrade.com/

Appendix – Links of Interest

Modern Healthcare - http://www.modernhealthcare.com/

Modern Materials Handling - http://www.mmh.com/

Nation's Restaurant News - http://nrn.com/

Packaging Digest - http://www.packagingdigest.com/

Packaging World - http://www.packworld.com/

Plastics News - http://www.plasticsnews.com/

Printing Impressions - http://www.piworld.com/

Public Works - http://www.pwmag.com/

Qualified Remodeler - http://www.forresidentialpros.com/

R&D Magazine - http://www.rdmag.com/

Realty Times - http://realtytimes.com/

Roads & Bridges - http://www.roadsbridges.com/

Site Selection - http://www.siteselection.com/

Traditional Building - http://www.traditional-building.com/

Trustee - http://www.trusteemag.com/

University Business - http://www.universitybusiness.com/

Training

Dale Carnegie Training - http://www.dalecarnegie.com/

PSMJ Resources – http://www.psmj.com

Society for Marketing Professional Services – http://www.smps.org

Toastmasters International - http://www.toastmasters.org/

Zweig Group – http://www.zweiggroup.com/

About the Author

Scott D. Butcher, FSMPS, CPSM is vice president and CMO of JDB Engineering, Inc. and affiliate companies. He has more than two decades of experience in A/E/C marketing, and is a Fellow of the Society for Marketing Professional Services and Certified Professional Services Marketer. An author of thirteen books, Scott is also a regular contributor to industry publications, writes the Marketropolis blog on the *Engineering News-Record* website, and co-authored the SMPS Foundation book *A/E/C Business Development - The Decade Ahead*. He's also served as president of the SMPS Foundation, board member of AIA Central PA Chapter, president of Historic York, Inc., and has been involved with numerous community and professional organizations. A regular presenter to professional associations and community groups, Scott resides in York, PA with his wife, Deborah, and their son, Jonathan. Learn more at www.scottbutcher.com and find him on LinkedIn, Facebook, Twitter, or YouTube at scottdbutcher.

www.ingramcontent.com/pod-product-compliance
Lightning Source LLC
Chambersburg PA
CBHW051856170526
45168CB00001B/129